Soldiers of the Revolutionary War Buried in Vermont

And Anecdotes and Incidents
Relating to Some of Them.

A paper read before the Vermont Historical Society in the
Hall of the House of Representatives, October 27, 1904,

By Walter H. Crockett.

CLEARFIELD

Excerpted from the
Proceedings of the Vermont Historical Society
1903-1904 and *1905-1906*

Reprinted with Permission
Genealogical Publishing Co., Inc.
Baltimore, Maryland, 1973

Reprinted for
Clearfield Company, Inc. by
Genealogical Publishing Co., Inc.
Baltimore, Maryland
1991, 1996, 2003

Library of Congress Cataloging in Publication Data
Crockett, Walter Hill, 1870-1931.
 Soldiers of the Revolutionary War buried in Vermont, and anecdotes
and incidents relating to some of them.
 "Excerpted and reprinted from Proceedings of the Vermont Histor-
ical Society, 1903-1904, 1905-1906.
 1. Vermont—History—Revolution. 2. United States—History—Rev-
olution—Registers, lists, etc. 3. Pensions, Military—United States—
Revolution.
 I. Title.
E255.C93   1973   929'.3743   72-10552
ISBN 0-8063-0534-7

Made in the United States of America

SOLDIERS OF THE REVOLUTION BURIED IN VERMONT, AND ANECDOTES AND INCIDENTS RELATING TO SOME OF THEM.

By WALTER H. CROCKETT.

In accordance with a resolution adopted at the last annual meeting of the Vermont Society, Sons of the American Revolution, held at St. Albans, Nov. 11, 1903, which authorized an attempt to ascertain as nearly as might be possible, the number of Revolutionary soldiers buried in this State, a request for information was made by the Secretary through the Vermont newspapers. Several hundred replies were received, not only from all parts of this State, but from nearly every section of the United States. Other names have been secured from Vermont gazetteers and histories.

Members of the Society of the Daughters of the American Revolution have taken a keen interest in this work, and from their replies and from the year books of their society many names have been secured. The largest number of names, however, has been found in a very rare copy of a list of Vermont Revolutionary pensioners, published many years ago, and secured by Senator Redfield Proctor.

In all, 4,608 names have been compiled. Entire accuracy cannot safely be claimed for a list gathered from such miscellaneous sources, with little opportunity for verification. Some names may be credited to the wrong town. The names of others who afterward removed from the

State may appear in the list. Care has been taken to make the compilation as accurate as possible, and in the main it will be found correct.

The pension list referred to is given by counties only, not by towns, and at the time of its compilation Lamoille County had not been organized.

Three divisions are given: First, a list of invalid pensioners; second, pensioners under the act of March 18, 1818; and third, pensioners under the act of June 7, 1832. A letter from the commissioner of pensions, the Hon. Eugene F. Ware, states that all the beneficiaries under the acts referred to were Revolutionary soldiers. The State in whose service each soldier enlisted is given, but not the regiment.

The names of 3,196 soldiers are given as pensioners. Windsor County leads with 546, while Rutland County is second with 479. Out of the 3,196 pensioners mentioned, only 172, or a little more than 5 percent., served in the Vermont militia. Nearly one-half—1,409, to be explicit—served in Massachusetts regiments; Connecticut contributed 701; New Hampshire, 444; Rhode Island, 104; New York, 75, and there were a few from other states, besides a number of naval veterans. These figures give an idea of the emigration into Vermont during the years immediately following the close of the Revolution.

There are, in the list compiled, the names of 2,221 soldiers who are accredited to the towns in which they lived and were buried. This number includes 809 names duplicated in the pension list. Deducting 809 names from the total pension list, there are left 2,387 names accredited only to counties, or a total of 4,608 soldiers of the Revolution who lived and died in Vermont.

Of the 246 towns and cities in the State, 192 are represented in the list. If the pension list given by counties could be given by towns, it is probable that nearly every town in the State would be found to contain the graves of Revolutionary soldiers.

Such a list, compiled nearly a century and a quarter after the close of the War for Independence, cannot possibly be complete. Some towns that naturally would be expected to furnish long lists send only a few names. If it is possible at this time to gather between 4,000 and 5,000 names, it is probable that nearly if not quite 6,000 soldiers of the Revolution found their last resting places within the borders of Vermont.

Manchester leads in the number of soldiers, reporting 241 names. Pawlet reports 71; Wilmington, 69; Barnard, 62; Dummerston, 49; Rutland, 49; Danby, 43; Newbury, 42; Pittsford, 41; Brattleboro, 38; Poultney, 34; Bennington, 31; Benson, 30; Fairfax, 29; Strafford, 30; Cornwall, 29; Randolph, 27; Reading, 26; Middletown Springs, 26; Middlebury, 25; Calais, 24; St. Albans, 23; New Haven, 23; Shoreham, 24; Salisbury, 22; Westminster, 41; Orwell, 21; Putney, 21; Clarendon, 21; Williamstown, 20; Barre, 20.

In prosecuting this investigation three real sons of the Revolution have been found in Vermont. Jonathan Babcock, of Stratton, aged 94 years, is the son of Robert Babcock, of Wardsboro, who died Aug. 23, 1863, at the great age of 104 years and 6 months. Robert Babcock was one of forty picked men who aided Lieut. Col. William Barton, of the Rhode Island militia (later the founder of Barton, Vt.) to capture Sir William Prescott, the British commander in Rhode Island. James C. Church, of Brookline, 85 years old, is the youngest of twenty children born to Charles Church, of Westminster, who enlisted as a soldier in the Revolutionary War when only 16 years old. Dr. C. A. Perry, of Readsboro, aged 66 years, must be one of the youngest real sons of the Revolution in the United States. His father, Micah Perry, of Concord, enlisted when 16 years old.

ANECDOTES AND INCIDENTS.

A few of the anecdotes related in the letters received by the Secretary may be of interest.

William Cox, of West Fairlee, Adam Beals, of St. Albans, and Lieut. John. Wyman, of Dummerston, were present at, and had a part in, the famous "Boston Tea Party," Dec. 16, 1773.

Capt. Thomas White, of Windsor, Thomas Townsend, of Reading, Thomas Farnsworth, of Halifax, Peletiah Bliss, of Newbury, Thomas Savery, of Salisbury, Jonas Holden, of Mount Holly, Seth Oaks and Nathaniel Oaks, of Athens, Seth Ruggles, of Poultney, Capt. John Shumway, of Dorset, Lieut. Jonathan Farrar, of Rupert, and Ebenezer Allen, of Newfane, were among those who responded to the Lexington alarm. The Ebenezer Allen mentioned was not the Col. Ebenezer Allen prominent in the expeditions of the Vermont militia.

Stephen De Maranville, of Poultney, the youngest son of a noble Frenchman, served as minute man. Jonathan Farrar, of Rupert, was a lieutenant of minute men at the time of the Lexington alarm. Thomas Mullen, of Newbury, responded to the Lexington alarm and saw service at Bunker Hill. Joseph Rann, of Poultney, was severely wounded at Bunker Hill, and to the day of his death carried a ball in his ankle received in that battle. Capt. Isaac Holden, of St. Albans, participated in the battles of Lexington and Bunker Hill and had previously served in the French and Indian War.

Carlos Hawkins, of Reading, Capt. Daniel Manning, of Poultney, William Doe, Nehemiah Lovewell, and Peter Martin, of Newbury, Abraham Townsend, of Berlin, Jonathan Childs, of Wilmington, Seth Oaks, of Athens, and Lieut. Beriah Sherman, of Waitsfield, fought in the battle of Bunker Hill. Jonas Holden, of Mount Holly, was wounded at Bunker Hill. Abial Bugbee, of Pomfret, served in Col. Israel Putnam's regiment at Bunker Hill.

It is related of William A. Hawkins, of Reading, that at the battle of Bunker Hill he fired his gun until it was too hot to handle. He removed his coat, wrapped it around the gun, and continued firing. He was promoted to be an ensign for gallant conduct in that battle.

Ebenezer Wakefield, of Manchester, was at Bunker Hill and at the surrender of Burgoyne. Luther Fairbanks, of Pittsfield, was at Bunker Hill and at the siege of Quebec. Capt. Elias Greene, of Cambridge, was at Bunker Hill, at the surrender of Burgoyne at Saratoga, and at the surrender of Cornwallis at Yorktown.

Col. Ephraim Doolittle, of Shoreham, who was with Lord Amherst at the capture of Ticonderoga and Crown Point during the French and Indian War, commanded a regiment of minute men April 19-23, 1775.

Maj. Amos Morrill, of St. Albans, is said to have been at the taking of Ticonderoga and at the battle of Bunker Hill. Other names of men said to have been with Ethan Allen at the capture of Ticonderoga, and not given in the

list published in the Burlington Free Press early in the present year by Robert O. Bascom, secretary of the New York
State Historical Association, are: John Alexander, of Brattleboro, Ebenezer Andrews, of Mount Holly, Gershom
Beach, of Salisbury, Enos Flanders, of Sheffield, Thomas
Johnson, of Newbury, Noah Jones, of Shoreham, and Samuel Laughton, of Dummerston.

Enoch Cheney, of Washington, and James Eddy, of
Clarendon, served as scouts. Ebenezer McIlvane suffered
the hardships of the terrible winter at Valley Forge. Felix
Benton, of Cornwall, wintered at Valley Forge and was on
duty as a picket when Major Andre was executed as a spy.
Hananiah Brooks, of St. Albans, was also at Valley
Forge, and later saw Major Andre hanged. Simeon Chand-
ler, of Wilmington, participated in the siege of Boston.

Jonathan Knight, of Dummerston, was in the fight at
the Westminster court house, March 13, 1775. Capt. Benjamin Samson, of Roxbury, rang the church bell at Lexington, Mass., April 19, 1775, to arouse the minute men
on the approach of the British troops.

John Chipman, of Middlebury, was with Ethan Allen
during the spring of 1775, went to Canada with Seth Warner, and was at the capture of St. Johns and Montreal.

Stephen Holley, of Cornwall, was with Benedict Ar-
nold on his terrible journey through Maine and Canada to
Quebec. Nathaniel Stedman, of Newfane, and Samuel
Viall, of Manchester, were at Burgoyne's surrender.

David Green, of Randolph, served three years under
General Washington, part of the time as his cook.

Joseph Allen, of Charlotte, was present at the capture
of St. Johns and Montreal, and was with Benedict Arnold
in his siege of Quebec.

Ebenezer Robinson, of Reading, was a captive on board the prison ship "Jersey" in New York harbor.

David Field, of Guilford, was commissary general under Gen. John Stark at the battle of Bennington.

Thomas Johnson, of Newbury, was an aide on the staff of General Lincoln in 1777.

Nathan Jackson, of Cornwall, was a trusted messenger of General Washington.

Benoni Gleason, of Benson, was present at the surrender of Lord Cornwallis at Yorktown.

Jonathan Martin, of Springfield, previous to removing to Vermont, was a member of the first constitutional convention and of the first legislature of New Hampshire.

Solomon Bartlett, of Plainfield, was the youngest brother of Josiah Bartlett of New Hampshire, after John Hancock the first signer of the Declaration of Independence, and was at one time an aide on the staff of General Israel Putnam.

Capt. John Warner and Truman Warner, of St. Albans, were brothers of Col. Seth Warner.

Col. Thomas Elmore obtained a charter for and gave his name to the town of Elmore.

Abel Amsden, of Reading, enlisted in Col. William Prescott's regiment, May 20, 1775. He participated in the siege of Boston, and fought in some of the most important battles of the war. It is related that he paid $70 in Continental currency for a dinner of corn bread and milk at a tavern, and that the landlord did not consider that sum a fair price for the meal.

Col. Samuel Brewer, of Orwell, was a lieutenant in a company of minute men raised in Berkshire County, Massachusetts, and took part in the siege of Boston. In 1776 he was sent to Ticonderoga in command of a regiment. In the Brewer genealogy, compiled by Prof. Fiske Parsons Brewer, a brother of Mr. Justice Brewer of the United States Supreme Court, it is said that Col. Brewer was "considered by Washington one of the biggest sensed men he ever knew." Colonel Brewer moved to Vermont and built a brick mansion a mile and half southwest of Orwell village, which is still in an excellent state of preservation.

Nathaniel Bosworth, of Berlin, while serving in the Continental army, was taken prisoner by the British and confined on a prison ship at the mouth of the Delaware river. Conceiving the idea that they were being slowly poisoned, Bosworth and several of his fellow-prisoners planned to escape. Taking advantage of a time when the guards were sleeping, they slid down the ship's cable and swam ashore, although the water was very cold, the month being March. Proceeding a distance, Bosworth concealed himself in a large cask and fell asleep. He was awakened by the singing of a bird. A patriotic American woman gave him food and directions which enabled him to reach the American lines in safety.

Toward the end of the war, Thomas M. Wright, who had seen service as a private in the Massachusetts militia, emigrated to Vermont and settled in Barnard, when that town was largely an unbroken wilderness. He built a log house and made a clearing. It was necessary to carry his grain on his back to Windsor, twenty-six miles, to get it ground, finding his way by marked trees and making the journey in a day. Aug. 9, 1780, Mr. Wright, while working in the hay field, heard a scream, and looking up saw his wife pursued by 25 Indians. The house was stripped of its furnishings and Mr. Wright was taken as a prisoner to Canada, where he was sold to the British for eight dollars. With four companions Wright made his escape. The party was nine days in coming through the forests. The men had no food except the game they shot, and were nearly starved. One of the party was taken ill and his companions stayed with him as long as they dared. To remain longer meant that all would perish, so a bed of boughs was made by a running stream, a store of slippery elm bark and roots was gathered, and the man left to his fate. Strangely enough he recovered, and in eighteen days came out of the forest. Mrs. Wright had gone on horseback to her father's home in Hardwick, and there her husband found her.

Dr. Silas Hodges, of Clarendon, was a surgeon in Washington's army. Another Clarendon soldier was Theophilus Harrington, later a judge, whose demand of a bill of sale from the Almighty for a fugitive slave has made his name immortal.

Stephen Hall, of Calais, enlisted in the American army at the age of 13, and Asa Wilson, of Fairfield, at the age of 14. Samuel White, of East Montpelier, enlisted before he had reached his 14th birthday. Not being considered old enough to carry a musket, he was detailed as a servant for General Washington.

Joshua Johnson, of Albany, when a boy, ran away from home to enlist. Being refused, he shipped as a midshipman in the West India trade and later entered the army, serving until the close of the war. It is related that in later years he defeated Ira Allen as a candidate for the Vermont Legislature from Irasburgh.

William Hodgkins, of Grand Isle, was not tall enough to meet the requirements of the service when he enlisted. Later he presented himself again, having filled his shoes with paper, evidently believing that by taking thought he might add a cubit to his stature, notwithstanding Scriptural authority to the contrary. The deception was discovered and the case brought to the attention of the commanding officer, Baron Steuben, who laughingly said, "Pass him in. We will make a drummer of him."

One of the surprising facts brought out by this investigation is the great age attained by many Revolutionary soldiers in this State, a large number having lived to be well past 90 years.

Samuel McWaine, of Woodstock, who had seen service in the French and Indian War, and who served seven years during the Revolution, lived to be 99 years and 9 months old.

John Ellis, of Barnard rounded out a full century. Nathan Lounsbury, of Clarendon, lived to be 102 years old. Daniel Heald, of Chester, who had taken part in the battle of Concord, lived to be 95 years old, while John Joyal, of Swanton, according to the best information obtainable, lived to the almost unprecedented age of 113 years.

One colored man, John Linde, of Brookfield, was a Revolutionary soldier.

It may not be out of place in this paper, which, from its nature cannot be expected to be a closely connected narrative, to refer briefly to a soldier who played an important part in the Revoluton, who afterward emigrated to Vermont, where he attained considerable prominence, but who has been well nigh forgotten, Col. Udny Hay.

The public papers of George Clinton, the first governor of New York, which cover the period of the Revolutionary War, contain a great amount of correspondence with Col. Hay, regarding supplies of various kinds and the transportation of the same. In 1779 he was deputy quartermaster general for the army in New York State. His task was evidently one of great difficulty, as the collection and distribution of the needed supplies was attended by irritating indifference and aggravating delays. One item in his report tells of the purchase of 40,000 bushels of charcoal for the smith's department. When General Washington ordered the Hudson river craft repaired it was Col. Hay who procured the lumber. General Lincoln wrote Hay asking his advice regarding the building of gunboats. He also wrote Generals Greene and Heath regarding the purchase of wheat. Apparently he had charge at times of certain prisoners and their effects.

In June, 1780, Colonel Hay was appointed agent for New York to supply the State's quota of provisions for the use of the army, and he writes: "Much of the business of transportation in this State may probably come under my direction during the campaign." Again he writes Governor Clinton: "The army look up to me for the transportation of supplies of every sort," and later the governor refers to the multiplicity of affairs which engage Hay's attention. He aids in reinforcing West Point, forwards supplies to Washington's army, and obtains from the New York Legislature the passage of certain acts to aid him in collecting supplies. Appointed deputy commissary general of purchases for New York, he recommends the establishment of a magazine of 40,000 barrels of flour for the army.

Sept. 18, 1780, he writes Governor Clinton: "I have been with the Gentlemen of the New Hampshire Grants at Bennington who have desired me to meet them again next Friday at the same place where they are to call a council for the purpose of giving me every assistance in their power, which I now apprehend will be but little, not from want of inclination, but want of ability to putt any of their acts in execution."

According to a statement in "Governor and Council," Colonel Hay had visited Bennington on a similar errand early in 1778. This authority further states that Col. Hay was descended from an eminent family in Scotland, and was highly educated. January 9, 1777, the Continental Congress resolved that Udny Hay, Esq., be appointed a lieutenant colonel by brevet and assistant deputy quartermaster general, and stationed at Ticonderoga. Later he was made deputy commissary general of purchase for the northern division of the army. Soon after the close of the war he came to Underhill, where he acquired large tracts of land. He represented the town in the legislature from 1798 to 1804 and at the time of his death was a member of the Council of Censors. He is said to have been opposed to the Constitution and to the administrations of Washington and Adams.

An obituary notice in the Burlington Sentinel tells of Colonel Hay's death Sept. 6, 1806, in his 67th year. A note in "Governor and Council" states that he lived and died in Underhill, but the Sentinel declares that his death "took place in this town [Burlington] * * * after a very short illness * * * The next day [Sept. 7th] his remains were conveyed to the meeting house, where an appropriate discourse was delivered by the Rev. President Sanders and attended to the grave by a numerous and respectable procession of his friends from this and the neighboring towns with uncommon manifestations of regard for his character and sorrow at his death."

The obituary notice further says: "Col. Hay came to America without education, without property or friends. During our Revolutionary war he soon and long distinguished himself in the department where he was stationed as an active, enterprising and able officer. And since the establishment of our State, his influence in our public councils for a considerable number of years has been predominant beyond a parallel." It will be noticed that there are discrepancies between the two accounts of Colonel Hay's career, as given in the Sentinel and in "Governor and Council." It appears from a further item in the Sentinel that Colonel Hay's estate was insolvent.

If Colonel Hay's grave can be found it should be marked in some suitable way. It would appear from the Sentinel account that he was buried in Burlington, but the list of Revolutionary soldiers kept by the Burlington Grand Army Post does not contain Colonel Hay's name.

One of the principal objects in the attempt to compile a list of Vermont's Revolutionary soldiers, is the hope that as many as possible of the graves of these heroes may be marked and their memories saved from oblivion.

The government will furnish headstones for such graves and ship them to the nearest railway station, but will not set them. Here is a work, not only for the patriotic societies, but for public-spirited citizens in all towns and cities where Revolutionary soldiers are buried,—the work of taking the proper steps to secure such headstones and then setting them after they are obtained. These soldiers of the Revolution were the builders of our State and of our Nation. The very least we can do in return for their sacrifices is to see to it that their names are not forgotten. Any work that is to be done along this line must be done speedily. No great outlay of time or money is required—only that patriotic public spirit that gives promise of a noble future because of its jealous care in preserving the memory of the great deeds of the past.

REVOLUTIONARY SOLDIERS INTERRED IN VERMONT.

ADDISON.

Lieut. Benjamin Adams
Daniel Champion
Sylvanus Chapin
Capt. —— Cook
Lieut. Benjamin Everest
Capt. Zadock Everest
Maj. T. Woodford

ALBANY.

Joshua Johnson

ANDOVER.

Ebenezer Cox
Reuben Kendall

ALBURG.

William Bell
Capt. Benjamin Marvin
Matthew Niles

ARLINGTON.

Israel Canfield

ATHENS.

Seth Oaks
Josiah Powers
James Shafter

BARNARD.

Solomon Aikens
James Allen
Lemuel Ashley
Abel Babbitt
Thomas Badford

Elijah Barnes
Moses Belden
Amos Bicknell
Gideon Billings
Aaron Blanchard
Joseph Bowman
Ephraim Briggs
Asa Brigham
Matthew Brown
Joseph Chamberlin
Benjamin Clapp
Ebenezer Cox
George Cox
Shiverick Crowell
John Cummings
Joel Davis
Seth Dean
Benjamin Eastman
Timothy Eastman
John Ellis
Joseph Ellis
Aaron Fay
Calvin Fairbanks
John Fish
John Foster
Joseph Foster
Thomas Freeman
Roger French
John Gambel
Nathaniel Haskell
Jesse Kinney
Jacob Lawton
Jacob Learned
Enoch Leonard
Ebenezer Lewis
Jonathan Luce
Moses Lurvey
Gideon Newton

John Newton
Timothy Newton
Asa Paige
George Paige
Nathaniel Paige
Amaziah Richmond
Lemuel Richmond
Nathaniel Richmond
Walker Richmond
Daniel Sharpe
Christopher Smith
Stewart Southgate
Andrew Stevens
Lieut. Elias Stevens
Asa Whitcomb
Jabez Wight
Jonathan Wight
Nathaniel Wight
Thomas M. Wright

BARNET.

Joseph Bonett
Thomas Clark
George Gibson
Joseph Goodwillie
Amasa Grout
Daniel Hall
Archibald Harvey
Thomas Haseltine
William Johnson
John McLaren
James Orr
Bartholomew Somers
Caleb Stiles
Sergt. William Strobridge
William Tice
———— Wilson
John Woods

BARRE.

Zebedie Beckley
Maj. William Bradford
James Briton
Abel Camp
Gould Camp
Lieut. Lemuel Clark
Francis Davis
Nathaniel Brown Dodge
Warren Ellis

Nathan Harrington
Abijah Holden
Nathaniel Holden
Serg't Jonas Nichols
Robert Parker
Asahel Paterson
Capt. Asaph Sherman
Nathaniel Sherman
Molton Stacy
Adolphus Thurston
Lieut. Benjamin Walker

BARTON.

John Merriam
Serg't Samuel Wells

BELLOWS FALLS.

Charles Church

BENNINGTON.

Hezekiah Armstrong
Hopestil Armstrong
James Bushnell
Robert Blair
Nathan Clark, Jr.
John Crawford
Elijah Dewey
David Fay
Elijah Fay
John Fay
Jonas Fay
Nathaniel Fillmore
Josiah Fuller
Anthony Haswell
Eleazer Hawks
Simeon Hathaway
Thomas Henderson
Capt. Samuel Herrick
Aaron Hubbell
Elnathan Hubbell
John Norton
Shadrack Norton
David Robinson
Joseph Robinson
Moses Robinson
Samuel Robinson
Joseph Rudd
Ephraim Smith
Henry Walbridge

Isaac Webster
Joseph Wickwire

BENSON.

Abel Bacon
Capt. William Barber
Christopher Bates
John Carter
Jonah Carter
Solomon Chittenden
Lieut. Stephen Crofoot
Capt. Joel Dickinson
Serg't John Dunning
Walter Durfee
Capt. William Ford
Solomon Gibbs
Allen Goodrich
Lieut. Caleb Goodrich
Simeon Goodrich
Thomas Goodrich
Benoni Gleason
Jacob Gleason
Maj. Osias Johnson
William Jones
Rev. Dan Kent
Allen Leet
William Manning
Lieut. Solomon Martin
James Noble
Amos Root, Jr.
John Stearns
Asahel Stiles
Jacob Thomas
Reuben Wilkenson

BÉRKSHIRE.

Elias Babcock
Job L. Barber
Capt. Phineas Heath
William Larrabee
Capt. David Nutting
Maj. Stephen Royce
Benjamin B. Searles

BERLIN.

Richard Bailey
Nathaniel Bosworth
James Braman
William Flagg
John Flanders

Joseph Goodenow
Serg't David Nye
Elijah Nye
Solomon Nye
James Parley
Zachariah Perrin
Stephen Person
Capt. James Sawyer
Thomas Spears
Capt. Daniel Taylor
Abraham Townsend

BETHEL.

Silas Adams
Serg't Elisha A. Fowlei
James Huntington
Thomas McKnight
John Moody
Sylvanus Owen
Samuel Paine
Jonathan Rice
Godfrey Richardson
William Wight

BOLTON.

Samuel Barnet
John Kennedy

BRAINTREE.

Serg't Samuel Bass
Enoch Cleveland
Exter Doleby
Daniel Flint
Serg't Jonathan Flint
Phineas Flint
Elijah French
John Gooch
Seth Mann
Lieut. Isaac Nichols
David Smith
Jeremiah Snow
Ebenezer White

BRADFORD.

Samuel Aspinwall
Theodore Barker
Col. John Barron
Bliss Corliss
Emerson Corliss

Capt. Robert Hunkins
Reuben Martin
James McFarlin

BRANDON.

Jonas Bagley
Samuel Burnell
Edward Cheney
Jacob Farrington
Joshua Field
Nathan Flint
David Jacobs
Philip Jones
Jabez Lyon
John McCollom
David Merriam
Roger Starkweather
Jedediah Winslow

BRATTLEBORO.

John Alexander
Thomas Ackley
John Barnes
Samuel Bennett
Joel Bolster
William Butterfield
Benjamin Chamberlain
Oliver Chapin
Reuben Church
Jabez Clark
James Dennis
Benajah Dudley
Obadiah Gill
Daniel Harris
Salathiel Harris
William Harris
Elisha Hotchkiss
Bromer Jenks
Elias Jones
Income Jones
Israel Jones
Oliver Jones
Lieut. Joseph Joy
John Kelsey
Cushing King
Ichabod King
William King
Thaddeus Miller
Isaac Pratt

Serg't Hezekiah Salisbury
Nathaniel Sampson
Sylvanus Sartwell
Levi Shumway
Thomas Simpson
Lemuel Thompson
Royall Tyler
Samuel Wellington
David Wells

BRIDGEWATER.

Jonathan Capron

BRIDPORT.

Abraham Lawrence

Capt. Benjamin Miner
David Whitney
James Wilcox

BRISTOL.

Serg't John Bush
Lieut. Amaziah Hawkins
Serg't Robert Holley
Henry McLaughlin
Capt. Gurden Munsill

BROOKLINE.

Daniel Benson
Ebenezer Harwood
Samuel Rist
Jotham Stebbins
Timothy Wellman
Richard Whitney
Jonathan Wooley

BROOKFIELD.

Samuel Bagley
Serg't Asahel Durkee
Amasa Edson
Amaziah Grover
John Linde
Joseph Morse
Noah Paine
Edmund Pease
John Slade
Capt. Solomon Smith

Elisha Wilcox
Gershom York

BRUNSWICK.

Philip Grapes
Nathaniel Wait

BURLINGTON.

Col. Ebenezer Allen
Gen. Ethan Allen
Heman Allen
Capt. Lemuel Bradley
Capt. Alexander Catlin
Dr. Seth Cole
Gen. Roger Enos
Col. Udny Hay
Comfort Hicks
Capt. Jesse Hollister
Capt. Russell Jones
Samuel Page
Col. Stephen Pearl
John Pomeroy
Col. Nathan Rice
Serg't David Russell
Capt. Benjamin Russell
Stephen Russell
Capt. William Russell
James Sawyer
John Stacy

CABOT.

Lieut. David Blanchard
Trueworthy Durgin
Nathan Edson
Jonathan Heath
Starling Heath
Maj. Lyman Hitchcock
Lieut. Fifield Lyford
Lieut. Thomas Lyford
Jerry McDaniels
Thomas Osgood
Samuel Warner
Nathaniel Webster
Lieut. John Whittier

CALAIS.

William Abbott
Welcome Ainsworth

John Battist
Joshua Bliss
Jonas Cousins
Seth Doan
David Fuller
Backus Gary
Ebenezer Goodenough
Stephen Hall
Moses Haskell
Nathaniel Jacobs
Francis Le Barron
Job Macomber
John Martin
Phineas Slayton
Jesse Slayton
Shubael Shortt
Ezekiel Sloan
Richard Ringe
Serg't Samuel White
Asa Wheelock
Edmund Willis
Duncan Young

CAMBRIDGE.

Jonah Brewster
Capt. Frank Greene
Elias Greene
Nathaniel Read
David Safford

CASTLETON.

Darius Branch
Lieut. Rufus Branch
Col. Isaac Clark
Eli Coggswell
Peter Cogswell
Jonathan Dunning
Cyrus Gates
Capt. John Hall
Lieut. Elias Hall
Nehemiah Hoit
Col. Noah Lee
Zadock Remington

CAVENDISH.

Timothy Fulham
John Spaulding

CHARLOTTE.

Lieut. Joseph Allen
Samuel Andrews
Lamberton Clark
Levi Coggswell
Samuel Hadlock
James Hill
Serg't Daniel Hosford
David Hubbell
Phineas Lake
Skiff Morgan
Asa Naramore
Elisha Pulford
Newton Russell
Israel Sheldon
Joseph Simonds
Ezra Wormwood

CHELSEA.

Ebenezer Allen
Laban Brown
Serg't Jonas Gates
Samuel Hayward
Samuel Lincoln
Thomas Moore
Enos Smith
Elkanah Stevens

CHITTENDEN.

Josiah Pearson
Jonathan Wood

CHESTER.

George Earl
Daniel Heald

CLARENDON.

Lieut. Samuel Allen
William Carpenter
Moses Chaplin
Levi Colvin
Zebulon Crane
William Crossman
David Dean
James Eddy
Joseph Fields
Benjamin Foster
Theophilus Harrington

Gideon Hewitt
Dr. Silas Hodges
Nathan Lounsbury
Samuel Newton
John Smith
Perry Smith
Abel Titus
Lieut. Col. Joseph Wait
Serg't Richard Weaver
Silas Whitney

COLCHESTER.

Elisha Allen

CONCORD.

David Hibbard
Micah Perry
Jonathan Woodbury

CORINTH.

Ebenezer Barry
Amos Boardman
Jeremiah Bowen
Abel Jackman
Peter V. Mahew
Reuben Page
Daniel Stevens
Bracket Towle

CORNWALL.

Seth Abbott
Roger Amy
Eldad Andrus
Zachariah Benedict
Felix Benton
Jeremiah Bingham
Samuel Blodgett
Abijah Davis
Benajah Douglass
Daniel Foot
Hiland Hall
Ambrose Hill
Stephen Holley
Elisha Hurlburt
William Hurlburt
Samuel Ingraham
Nathan Jackson
Jonathan Jennings
Israel C. Jones

David Parkhill
Jacob Peck
Lieut. Benjamin Reeve
Samuel Richards
William Slade
Ebenezer Stebbins
Benjamin Stevens
Calvin Tilden
Abraham Williamson
Moses Wooster

COVENTRY.

Amasa Wheelock

DANBY.

Ephraim Briggs
John Brock
John Bromley
Joshua Bromley
William Bromley
Rufus Bucklin
Capt. John Burt
Joseph Button
Capt. Stephen Calkins
Dennis Canfield
Abraham Chase
Jonathan Crandall
David Comstock
Obadiah Edmunds
Benedict Eggleston
Henry Frost
Capt. William Gage
Israel Harrington
Thomas Harrington
Henry Herrick
Henry Lewis
Peter Lewis
Elisha Lincoln
Darius Lobdell
Lieut. Abraham Locke
Jonathan Mabbitt
Ephraim Mallory
Jabeth Matteson
Gideon W. Moody
Lieut. John Mott
Israel Phillips
Israel Priest
Isaac Reed
William Roberts
Joseph Ross

Israel Seley
Jonathan Seley
Gideon Taber
Water Taber
Capt. Micah Vail
Capt. John Vail
Isaac Wade
Capt. Ebenezer Wilson

DANVILLE.

Eli Bickford
Jacob Chamberlain
Samuel Chamberlain, Jr.

DORSET.

Jonathan Armstrong
Reuben Bloomer
Jonathan Crandall
Justus Holley
William Manley
Stephen Martindale
Cephas Kent
Cephas Kent, Jr.
Prince Paddock
Capt. John Shumway
Maj. Simeon Smith
Nathaniel Viall
Capt. Abraham Underhill

DOVER.

Serg't Elijah Baldwin
Joseph Briggs
David Dexter
Gamaliel Ellis
William Hall
Samuel Hill
Gardner Howe
Joshua Kendall
David Leonard
Abner Perry
Ebenezer Sears
Ebenezer Sparks
Luther Ward
Timothy Wood

DUMMERSTON.

Nathan Adams
Joseph Bemis
Joshua Bemis

David Bennett
Stewart Black
Isaac Boyden
Maj. Josiah Boyden
Ebenezer Brooks
Elijah Brown
Elijah Buck
Jabez Butler
John Burnham
James Chase
William Cummings
Jason Duncan
Asa Dutton
Benjamin Estabrook
William French
Daniel Gates
Elijah Gibbs
Joseph Gilbert
Benjamin Gleason
John Gould
James Hanley
Joseph Hilliard
Arad Holton
Daniel Houghton
Seth Hudson
Jonathan Huntley
Josiah Kellogg
Joel Knight
Jonathan Knight
John Laughton
Nathaniel Laughton
Samuel Laughton
Daniel Lester
Serg't Calvin Munn
Capt. Isaac Miller
John Miller
Maj. Joseph Miller
John Negus
Samuel Norcross
Benjamin Pierce
Elkanah Prentice
Lemuel Presson
Lieut. Leonard Spaulding
Isaac Taylor
Joshua Wilder
Lieut. John Wyman

DUXBURY.

Serg't John Cabot
Benjamin Davis

David Phelps
Samuel Ridley

EAST MONTPELIER.

Enoch Cate
Theophilus Clark
Roland Edwards
Serg't John Gray
Job Macomber
Elias Metcalf
John Putnam
David Russell
Daniel Russell
Joshua Sanders
Samuel Southwick
Clark Stevens
Hezekiah Tinkham
Edward West
Samuel White

ÉLMORE.

Col. Samuel Elmore

ENOSBURG.

William Boyd
Jacob Baker
William Cragie
Ebenezer Dunham
Seth Denio
Ephraim Leach
James Hall
John Perley
Nathaniel Sherman
Maj. Benjamin Williams

ESSEX.

Jonathan Bixby
Lieut. Samuel Bradley
Stephen Butler
Thomas Chipman
Gideon Curtis
David Day
William Ingraham
Abram Stevens

FAIRFAX.

Briar Beeman
Philip Blaisdell

Josiah Brush
Anthony Cline
James Crissey
Stephen England
Asa Farnsworth
James Farnsworth
Oliver Farnsworth
Oliver Farwell
Jonathan George
Edmund Goodrich
Stephen Howard
Stephen Holmes
Arad Jay
James Keeler
Zelda Keyes
Hampton Lovegrove
Jonathan Major
Jedediah Merrill
Joseph Merrill
Nathan Murray
Brigham Rood
Joseph Starkweather
Thomas Stickney
Jacob Story
Bernard Ward
Isaac Webster
Robert Wilkins

FAIRFIELD.

Josiah Briggs
Serg't John Colburn
John B. Mitchell
Phinehas Page
Medad Parson
Francis Story
Oscar Wilson
Benjamin Wooster

FAIR HAVEN.

Jacob Barnes
Jonathan Cady
Solomon Cleaveland
Serg't Isaac Cutler
Alexander Dunohue
William Dutton
Ezra Hamilton
Oliver Kidder
Gamaliel Leonard
Noah Priest

Serg't Ethan Whipple
Dr. James Witherell

FAIRLEE.

Francis Churchill
Lieut. Ebenezer Cook
Benjamin Follett
Samuel Woods
Asa Woodward

FAYSTON.

Ebenezer Cutler
Joseph Marble
Jesse Mix
William Wait

FERRISBURG.

Reuben Martin
Noah Porter

FLETCHER.

Thomas L. Munsil
Briggs Rood

FRANKLIN.

Maj. Leonard Keep
Col. Ebenezer Marvin
Capt. Lemual Roberts
William Sisco
James Stevenson
Reuben Towle

GEORGIA.

Elisha Bartlett
Samuel Bartlett
Frederick Cushman
Abram Laflin
Abel Parker
Abel Pierce 2nd
William Post
Ethiel Scott
Joseph Stannard

GLASTENBURY.

Joshua Elwell

GOSHEN.

Phineas Blood
James Cowen
Reuben Grandey
Abiather Pollard

GRAND ISLÉ.

Isaac Adams
Joseph Adams
Lieut. Samuel Allen, Jr.
Ephraim Duell
Serg't Alpheus Hall
William Hazen
William Hodgkins
Elijah Hyde
Jedediah Hyde
Grindal Reynolds
Daniel Wadsworth

GRANVILLE.

Isaac Cady
Levi Ball

GROTON.

Abraham Alexander
David Bachelder
Ebenezer Bachelder
Jeremiah Bachelder
Dominicus Gray
Jesse Heath
Jonathan Macomber
Samuel Randall
Edmund Welch

GUILFORD.

Benjamin Carpenter
David Field
Elisha Field
John Kent
John Shepardson

HALIFAX.

Thomas Farnsworth
Serg't Samuel Stafford

HANCOCK.

Obadiah Lamb

HARDWICK.

Capt. John Doe
———— Goss
———— Sinclair
Serg't John Stevens
Andrew Wheatley

HARTFORD.

Samuel Bailey
Sherebiah Ballard
William Champlin
Nathan Cobb
Joseph Fenno
Seth Fuller
Joseph Gallup
Roger Huntington
Elijah Kibbie
Christopher Pease
Burphy Prouty
Phineas Russ
Stephen Tilden
Elisha Woodard
William Whitman
Dr. James Wolcott

HARTLAND.

Amasa Bryant
Joseph Evans
John Orcutt
Sergt. Jeremiah Richardson
Moses Webster

HIGHGATE.

Ebenezer Chamberlin
John E. Johnson
Serg't Benjamin Story Meigs
Matthew Morehouse
Nathan Record

HINESBURGH.

David Beach
George Palmer

HUBBARDTON.

John Churchill
Samuel Churchill
Silas Churchill

Frederick Dikeman
Capt. Benjamin Hickok
Rev. Ithamer Hibbard
John Rumsey
William Rumsey
Jonathan Slayson
Serg't Asahel Wright
Capt. James Whelpley

HUNTINGTON.

James Ambler
Ebenezer Ambler
Serg't Solomon Buel
Charles Brewster
Benjamin Derby
John Fitch
Benjamin Holly
Jehiel Johns
Joshua Remington
Jacob Snyder

HYDE PARK.

Thomas Coote
Samuel Eaton
Darius Fitch
Capt. Jabez Fitch
Ephraim Garvin
Jacob Hadley
Capt. Jedediah Hyde
Lieut. Aaron Keeler
Capt. Peter Martin
Amos McKinstry
Jabez Newland
Oliver Noyes
Roger Toothaker

IRA.

Salmon Kingsley
Jason Newton
David Parker
Peter Parker
Nathaniel Wilmarth

ISLE LA MOTTE.

Daniel Bixby
Serg't William Blanchard
Serg't John Fadden
Nathaniel Hall

Caleb Hill
Abram Knapp
Ezra Pike
Elisha E. Reynolds
Henry Scott
Seth Strong
Gardner Wait
Joseph Willams
William Wilsey

JERICHO.

Thomas Barney
Lewis Chapin
John Lyman
Roderick Messenger

JOHNSON.

Samuel Eaton

LEICESTER.

Serg't John Barker
Capt. Thomas Sawyer
Stephen Sparks
Joseph Swinington

LINCOLN.

Owen Briggs
Wolcot Burnham
Ebenezer Durfy
Thomas Lee

LONDONDERRY.

Edward Aiken
Barach Bolster
William Cox
Samuel Davis
Hollis Eaton
John Hasey
Samuel Hayward
John Patterson
Benjamin Pierce
Thomas Reed
Nathaniel Shattuck
John Warner

LOWELL.

Hosea Sprague

LUNENBURGH.

Aaron Ames
Ebenezer Belknap
Warren Cook
Zerubbabel Eager
Levi Fay
Samuel Gates
Franklin Littlefield
Samuel Phelps
Moses Quimby
Lieut. ――― Rice
John Whipple

LYNDON.

Serg't Abel Carpenter
William Harvey

MANCHESTER.

Daniel Abbott
John Abbott
Jonathan Aiken
John Allen
Jonathan Allen
Josiah Allen
Seth Allen
David Anderson
James Anderson
Robert Anderson
Daniel Arnold
John Austin
Absalom Baker
Joseph Baker
Eleazer Baldwin
Daniel Barber
Gideon Barber
Samuel Barto
Benjamin Bears
Lewis Beebe
William Bedel
Nathan Beman
Samuel Beman
Jonathan Benedict
Samuel Benedict
William Bennett
Samuel Biney
Capt. Peter Black
Elijah Bliss
Timothy Bliss
Elijah Blodgett

Bernard Bourn
Jared Bourn
Nathaniel Bourn
Arthur Bostwick
Israel Bostwick
Nathaniel Bostwick
Jonathan Boyden
Christopher Brackett
James Breakenridge
Capt. Allen Briggs
David Brooks
Asa Brownson
Eli Brownson
Thomas Bull
Thomas Bull, Jr.
Joseph Bulkley
Charles Bullis
Henry Bullis
Beverly Burch
Joseph Burr
Elijah Burton
Isaac Burton, Jr.
Josiah Burton
James Cadwell
Abner Chaffee
Daniel Champion
Calvin Chamberlin
Amos Chipman
Ebenezer Clark
Josiah Clark
Robert Cochran
Elijah Cook
Elisha Cook
Charles Collins
Christopher Collins
Nathaniel Collins
Richard Colvin
Jonathan Corey
James Cowden
Hall Curtis
David Cutting
John Daggett
Shadrack Danks
Job Dean
Eliakim Dening
William Drew
Nathan Eaton
James Eddy
John Elliot
John Ells

Waterman Ells
Abel Emmons
Zadock Everest
Stephen Farman
Thomas Farr
Asa Farrand
Benjamin Fassett
John Fassett, Jr.
David Fay
Joseph Fay
John Forbes
Roswell Francis
Thomas French
Elijah French
Joseph French
Samuel French
Silas Goodrich
Zebedee Goodwin
William Gould
Jesse Graves
Thaddeus Harris
John Harris
John Hageboom
Barnabas Hatch
Cornelius Havens
Edward Henderson
Thomas Hill
William Hill
Simeon Hine
David Hix
Capt. Elijah Hollister
John Hopkins
John Howard
Samuel Hull
James Jameson
Daniel Jones
David Jones
John Langdon
Loren Larkin
Joseph Larkins
David Leavenworth
David Lee
David Lee, Jr.
James Lewis
Josiah Lockwood
Hugh Logan
John Logan
Robert Logan
Benjamin McIntyre
Joseph McIntyre

Isaac Marks
Aaron Mason
Benjamin Matteson
James Mead
Philip Mead
Timothy Mead
Timothy Mead, Jr.
Truman Mead
Zebulon Mead
Daniel Merriman
Daniel Miller
Noah Morse
Rufus Munson
Thaddeus Munson
James Murdock
Robert Nicholas
Jacob Odell
William Odel
Gideon Olmstead
Daniel Ormsby
Gideon Ormsby
Jonathan Ormsby
John Page
Jonathan Page
Timothy Pearl
Abel Pettibone
Samuel Pettibone
Seth Pettibone
Abel Phelps
Martin Powell
Truman Powell
Benjamin Purdy
Benjamin Purdy, Jr.
Daniel Purdy
David Purdy
Reuben Purdy
Solomon Purdy
William Ramsey
Philip Reynolds
Amos Richardson
Andrew Richardson
John Richardson
Nathan Richardson
Serg't Israel Roach
Benjamin Roberts
Christopher Roberts
Daniel Roberts
John Roberts
Peter Roberts
William Roberts

Samuel Robinson
Joel Ross
William Ross
John Sabin
Jesse Sawyer
Aaron Saxton
George Saxton
John Sayer
John Scott
Daniel Shaw
Josiah Sheldon
Timothy Skinner
Abraham Smith
Frederick Smith
George Smith
Isaac Smith
John Smith
John Smith, Jr.
Nathan Smith
Noah Smith
Reuben Smith
Seth Smith
Stephen Smith
Mordecai Soper
Pelatiah Soper
Solomon Soper
Thomas Soper
Timothy Soper
Moses Sperry
John Stewart
Wallace Sunderland
James Sutherland
John Sutherland
Lem Sutherland
Samuel Sutherland
Jonathan Taylor
Moses Taylor
Ezra Thompson
David Tuttle
Benjamin Vaughan
James Vaughn
Samuel Viall
Jeremiah Wait
Thomas Wait
Perez Walton
Capt. —— Wakefield
Serg't Ebenezer Wakefield
Stephen Washburne
Giles Walcott
Isaac Whipley

Jeremiah Whipley
John White
Samuel Wilcox
Stephen Wilcox
Edmund Wood
Nicholas Wood
Enoch Woodbridge
John Woodworth
John Wright
Samuel Wright

MARLBORO.

Thomas Adams
Justus Aingus
Zarager Bartlett
Sylvester Bishop
Elijah Bruce
John Church
Timothy Mather
Timothy Tomlin
Jonathan Warren
William Williams
Nathaniel Whitney

MARSHFIELD.

Jacob Black
Daniel Bemis
Nathaniel Corbin
Jonas Cummings
Henry Dwinell
Joseph J. Eaton
John Pike
Jonathan Willis

MIDDLEBURY.

Harvey Bell
Eleazer Barrows
Nathan Case
John Chipman
David Chaffen
Edward Eels
Freeman Foot
Martin Foot
Philip Foot
Bethuel Goodrich
Lieut. Stephen Goodrich
William Goodrich
Lebbeus Harris

Aaron Hastings
Eben W. Judd
Abraham Kirby
Henry Keeler
Ebenezer Markham
Timothy Mathews
Samuel Mattocks
Gamaliel Painter
Jonathan Preston
Jabez Rogers
John Stewart
Ebenezer Sumner

MIDDLESEX.

Joseph Chapin
Cyrus Hill
James Hobart
Joseph Hutchins
Seth Putnam
—— Sloan
Lyman Tolman
Ebenezer Woodbury

MIDDLETOWN SPRINGS.

Gideon Buel
John Burnham
Hezekiah Clift
Peter Crocker
Phineas Clough
Thomas Clough
David Enos
Luther Filmore
Serg't David Griswold
Jonathan Griswold
Benjamin Haskins
Jonathan Haynes
Jonathan Hays
Benjamin Huckins
Elisha Hutchins
George Kilbourn
Thomas Korgan
Thomas Morgan
Azor Perry
Ezekiel Perry
Francis Perkins
Philo Stoddard
Caleb Smith
Serg't Joseph Spalding
David Thomas
John Woodworth

MILTON.

David Austin
Joseph Austin
Alpheus Hall
William A. Newman
William Powell

MONKTON.

Ashbel Dean
Josiah Lawrence
David Rusco
William Peck
Abel Peck
Serg't John Phinney

MONTGOMERY.

Capt. Joshua Clapp

MONTPELIER.

Jacob Davis
Perley Davis
Aaron Griswold
Estis Hatch
Micah Hatch
Timothy Hatch
Luther King
Iram Nye
Richard Paine
Samuel Patterson
Eliakim D. Persons
Capt. Stephen Rich
Reuben Russell
Joseph Woodworth
Ziba Woodworth
Timothy Worth

MORRISTOWN.

Joseph Burke
Samuel Cook
Nathan Gates
Crispus Shaw
Moses Weld

MOUNT HOLLY.

Ebenezer Andrews
Jonas Holden

MORETOWN.

Reuben Hanks
Bissell Phelps

MORGAN.

Samuel Elliott
Jacob Taylor

MOUNT TABOR.

Serg't James Hathaway
Ira Moulton
Walter Taber

NEWBURY.

Bancroft Abbott
Nathan Avery
John Barnett
Frye Bayley
Jacob Bayley
Gen. Jacob. Bayley
James Bayley
Capt. John G. Bayley
Maj. Joshua Bayley
Capt. Jabez Bigelow
Peletiah Bliss
Thomas Brock
Abiel Chamberlin
Sergt. Joseph Chamberlin
Moses Chamberlin
Remembrance Chamberlin
Richard Chamberlin
Asa Coburn
Joel Corbee
William Doe
John Eaton
Abner Fowler
Jacob Fowler
Lieut. Jonathan Goodwin
Jonathan Hadley
Nehemiah Hadley
Col. Joab Hoisington
Capt. Lemuel Holmes
Col. Robert Johnston
Capt. Thomas Johnson
Col. Jacob Kent
Jacob Kent, Jr.
Capt. Nehemah Lovewell
Peter Martin

Thomas Mellen
John Mills
John Mills, Jr.
William Peach
Gideon Smith
Capt. Simeon Stevens
William Wallace
Peletiah Watson

NEWFANE.

Ebenezer Allen
David Anger
Ward Eager
Lieut. Jonathan Park
Daniel Phillips
Nathaniel Stedman
Robert Timson

NEW HAVÉN.

Abram S. Abbott
Lieut. ——— Baldwin
Amos Bird
George W. Bisbee
Solomon Brown
Martin Crane
Thomas Dickinson
Martin Eno
Alonzo H. Field
Capt. Nathaniel Hall
Jonathan Hoyt
Seth Hoyt
Seth Langdon
Mathen Phelps
Simeon Porter
William Seymour
George E. Smith
Nathan Smith
Josiah Taylor
Augustus Tripp
Jesse Ward
Preserved Wheeler
Capt. William Wheeler

NEWPORT.

John Niles

NORTHFIELD.

Noah Benson
Ebenezer Fox

Joseph Gold
David Hedges
John Loyd
Eleazer Nichols
Silas Roys
Ananias Tubbs
Serg't Jason Winch

NORTH HERO.

Samuel Allen
Elisha Hibbard
Nathan Hutchins
Nathan Hutchins, Jr.
Jedediah P. Ladd

NORWICH.

Elihu Baxter
Capt. Paul Brigham
Joseph Cushman
Joseph Cummins
Peter Olcott
Joseph Loveland
Timothy Wilmot

ORANGE.

Alden Freeman
Simeon Judkins
Capt. —— Nelson

ORWELL.

Apollos Austin
Elias Bascom
Seth Benson
Ephraim Blood
Archibald Brewer
Samuel Brewer
Daniel Buell
Lemuel Clark
James Conkey
Samuel Griswold
Ebenezer Hulburd
Wheeler Martin
John Noble
Simeon North
John Pepper
Jacob Perkins
Eli Root
Jonas Royce
Pliny Smith

Timothy Squier
N. Richardson Stoddard

PAWLET.

Gideon Adams
Joseph Adams
John Allen
Nehemiah Allen
Parmelee Allen
Timothy Allen, Jr.
Elisha Averill
Lieut. Samuel Borden
Aaron Bennett
Salah Betts
Roswell Bennett
Christopher Billings
David Blakely
Daniel Branch
Ebenezer Broughton
Elijah Brown
Nathaniel Carver
Oliver Churchill
Elisha Clark
Robert Cox
Asa Denison
Jedediah Edgerton
Jacob Edgerton
Capt. Simeon Edgerton
Serg't Abiather Evans
William Fitch
Gideon Gifford
Ebenezer Gillia
Ebenezer Gould
Ezekiel Harmon
Serg't Nathaniel Hill
Asahel Hollister
Lieut. Elijah Hollister
Junett Hollister
Capt. James Hopkins
Daniel Hallett
Buckley Hutchins
Silas Jones
Oliver Loomis
James Leach
Judah Moffitt
Serg't Josiah Monroe
Simeon Pepper
Maj. Moses Porter
Capt. William Potter
Capt. James Pratt

Samuel Pratt
Joseph Priest
Jedediah Reed
Isaac Reed
Simeon Reed
John Risden
Daniel Risdon
Abel Robinson
Ephraim Robinson
Serg't John Sargent
George Rush
Capt. John Start
Serg't Peter Stevens
Samuel Stratton
Nathaniel Robinson
Jacob Sylus
Lieut. Eliel Todd
Seth Viets
Lieut. Daniel Welch
Nathan Williams
David Willey
Andrew Winchester
John Wiseman
John Wood
Henry Wooster

PANTON.

Peter Ferris
Edward Grandy
Elijah Grandy
Benjamin Holcomb
Philip Spalding
Phineas Spalding, Jr.

PEACHAM.

Samuel Chamberlain
William Chamberlain
Jonathan Elkins

PITTSFIELD.

Luther Fairbanks

PITTSFORD.

John Barnes
Israel Buck
Isaac Buck
Isaac Buck, Jr.
Capt. Benjamin Cooley
Caleb Cooley

Gideon Cooley
William Cox
Darius Crippen
Serg't Jonathan Deming
Noadiah Deming
Ebenezer Drury
Luther Drury
Ephraim Dunlap
Israel Ellsworth
Samuel Ellsworth
John Hitchcock
Asahel Hopkins
Ebenezer Hopkins
James Hopkins
Nehemiah Hopkins
Ebenezer Lyman
Stephen Mead
Silas Mosher
Jabez Olmstead
Abdon Owen
Abraham Owen
Edward Owen
Aaron Parsons
John Penfield
Serg't Milton Potter
Zachariah Rand
Zachariah Rand, Jr.
Jonathan Rowley, Jr.
Abel Stevens
Benjamin Stevens
Benjamin Stevens, Jr.
Daniel Stevens
Ephraim Stevens
Samuel Sheldon
John Woodward

PLAINFIELD.

John Bancroft
Solomon Bartlett
Lieut. Joshua Lawrence
Moses Reed

POMFRET.

Abial Bugbee
William Clements
Jeremiah Conant
Nathaniel Carpenter
Serg't John Dexter
Dexter Hawkins
Increase Hewitt

Adam Howard
Joshua Lazelle
John Miller
Abiel Morse
Robert Perry
Jeremiah Pratt
Samuel Snow
Thomas Vail
Charles Walcott
Frederic Ware
William Watrous

PLYMOUTH.

Francis Akeley

POWNAL.

Josiah Wright
Samuel Wright

POULTNEY.

Maj. Heber Allen
Capt. Elkanah Ashley
Thomas Ashley
Jeremiah Armstrong
William Buckland
Stephen De Maranville
Maj. Zebudiah Dewey
Bazaleel Farnum
Capt. John Grant
James Hooker
Thomas Hooker
William Hooker
Nehemiah Howe
Silas Howe
Abel Hubbard
Lindley Joslin
Josiah Lewis
William Lewis
Daniel Mallory
Daniel Manning
Joseph Manning
Ichabod Marshall
Joseph Marshall
John Owen
Samuel Prindle
Joseph Rann
John Richards
Zebulon Richards
Seth Ruggles

Lieut. James Smith
Jesse Soper
Capt. William Watson
William Wood
Oliver Wright

PUTNEY.

Daniel Adams
David Brown
Seth Corey
Abram Houghton
Elijah Houghton
Joshua Hyde
Zenas Hyde
Daniel Jewett
Elisha Johnson
Moses Johnson
———— Kathan
Serg't Daniel Martin
Aaron M. Martin
Isaac Palmer
John Smith
Ezekiel Pierce
Lieut. John Stovers
James Upham
George Ware
Ezekiel Wilson
Luke Wilson

RANDOLPH.

Benjamin Blodgett
Henry Blodgett
Sylvanus Blodgett
Jacob Cobb
William Corley
Stephen Fish
Lieut. John Goss
David Green
David Grow
Dyer Hebard
Stephen Herrick
Joseph Hobart
Elisha Lilley
John McIntyre
Nathan Nye
Solomon Orcutt
Jacob Parish
Adonijah Rogers
James Steele

Isaac Thayer
Ansel Tucker
Oliver Tyler
Samuel Upham
Lieut. Edward Waldo
Serg't Abner Washburn
Levi Wilder
Benjamin Woodworth

READING.

Abel Amsden
Moses Chaplin
George Clark
Aaron Darling
Oliver Davis
James Hall
Josiah Harris
Benjamin Hathorn
Nathan Hatch
Capt. William A. Hawkins
Jeremiah Johnson
Solomon Keyes
Gideon Kirtland
Thomas Nichols
——— Nutting
Serg't Abiah Rice
William Rist
Ebenezer Robinson
James Robinson
Benjamin Sawyer
Cornelius Sawyer
Amos Wetherbee
Daniel Wetherbee
Elijah Williams
Lieut. ——— White
Jeduthun Wyman

RICHFORD.

Enoch Carlton
Hezekiah Goff

RICHMOND.

Edward Allen
James Humphrey
William Wells

RIPTON.

Jabez Hendrick
John S. Kirby
Samuel S. Kirby

ROCHESTER.

Kiles Paul

ROXBURY.

Samuel Richardson
Stephen Rumney
Benjamin Samson
Jedediah Smith

ROYALTON.

Gideon Crandall
Ebenezer Dewey
John Hutchinson
Asa Perrin

RUPERT.

Lieut. Jonathan Farrar

RUTLAND.

Joseph Barney
William Barr
Obadiah Bass
Joseph Bateman
Nathaniel Beaman
Jonathan Bell
Capt. Joseph Bowker
Benjamin Cheney
James Claghorn
John Cook
Barzilla Dewey
Daniel Douglass
William Emerson
John Fenton
Seth Gorham
David Gleason
Nathaniel Gore
Asa Hale
Moses Hale
Jesse Hayden
Amos Himes
Ephraim Jackson
Joseph Kimball
Phinehas Kingsley
Lieut. Thomas Lee
Jesse Long
Levi Long
Benjamin Johnson
John McConnell

Samuel McConnell
James Mead
William Page
David Pattison
Joshua Pratt
Nathan Pratt
Issacher Reed
Joshua Reynolds
Luther Shaw
Cephas Smith
John Smith
Solomon Smith
Daniel Squires
Henry Strong.
Samuel Thrall
David Tuttle
Serg't Amos Weller
Obadiah Wheeler
Serg't Eleazer Wheelock
Wait Wright

RYEGATE.

Serg't Abiel Learned
Sylvester Learned

SALISBURY.

Gershom Beach
Salathiel Bump
Samuel Daniels
Josiah Farnham
George Griswold
John Holt
Christopher Johnson
Henry Keeler
Samuel Keep
John Morton
Joshua Mossman
Joel Newton
Daniel Noyes
Samuel Pierce
William Pratt
Thomas Savery
Eli Smead,
Jabez Spencer
Simeon Strong
Jonathan Wainwright
Abe Waterous
Daniel Whiting

SANDGATE.

Serg't Lewis Hurd

SHAFTSBURY.

Jabez Elwell
John Elwell
Moses Elwell
Jonas Galusha
Aaron Hewlett
Gideon Olin

SHEFFIELD.

Samuel Drown
Enos Flanders

SHELBURNE.

Serg't Ebenezer Barstow
Capt. Israel Burritt
John Callender
Asahel Nash
Richard Spear
Lieut. Peter Stearns
Moses Pierson
Uzal Pierson
Ziba Pierson
Nathan White

SHÉLDON.

Lieut. Francis Duclos
Elisha Sheldon
David Sloan
Elisha Smith
Benjamin Stearns
Capt. Robert Wood

SHERBURNE.

Josiah Ward

SHOREHAM.

Stephen Barnum
Thomas Barnum
Ebenezer Bush
Amos Callender
Noah Callender
Timothy F. Chipman
Col. Ephraim Doolittle
Gideon Jennings

Noah Jones
Pete Jones
William Jones
Elijah Kellogg
John Larrabee
Daniel Newton
Josiah Pond
David Ramsdell
Hopkins Rowley
Thomas Rowley
Thomas Rowley, Jr.
Eli Smith
Nathan Smith
Samuel Wolcott
Samuel Wolcott, Jr.
Elijah Wright

SPRINGFIELD.

Andrew Bradford
William Brown
James Chittenden
Paul Haywood
John Harris
Joseph Hodgman
Capt. William Holden
William Kirk
Richard Lee
Thomas Leland
Jonathan Martin
Matthew Pierce

SHREWSBURY.

Philemen Adams
Samuel Dennis
Stephen Eastman
Capt. John Kilmorn
Serg't William Lord
Samuel Low
Capt. Nathaniel Smith

SOUTH HERO.

Benjamin Adams
Thomas Dixon
Eleazer Martin
John Monte
Joseph Mott, Jr.
Jabez Rockwell
Capt. Ephraim Sawyer
David Wadsworth

ST. ALBANS.

Adam Beals
Haclatiah Bridges
Paul Brigham
Hananiah Brooks
Samuel Church 2nd
John Delaney
John Gates
Serg't Isaac Gibbs
Lieut. Isaac Holden
Ithiel Holdridge
William Isham
Jonathan Janes
Col. Stephen Keyes
Hezekiah Keeler
Robert Lovewell
Daniel B. Meigs
Maj. Amos Merrill
Noel Potter
Zepheniah Ross
Samuel Todd
Bates Turner
Capt. John Warner
Truman Warner

STARKSBORO.

George Bidwell
Nathaniel Chafee
Solomon Phillips
Oliver White

ST. GEORGE.

Jehial Isham

ST. JOHNSBURY.

Jonathan Arnold
Serg't Barnabas Barker
Capt. John Barker
Capt. Samuel Barker
Simeon Cobb
Jonas Flint
Daniel Fuller
Stephen Hawkins
John Ide
Lemuel Jenkins
Joel Roberts

STRAFFORD.

Levi Bacon
Peter Benson
Ezra Blaisdell
Lieut. Timothy Blake
Samuel Bliss
John P. Burroughs
Elias Carpenter
Samuel Eastman
Benjamin George
Job Haskell
Robert Haynes
James Hyde
Enoch Jenkins
Jacob Killinger
Oliver Ladd
Benjamin Lilley
David Miller
Joseph Norton
Azel Percival
Serg't John Powell
Jonathan Rich
David Rich
Jonathan Rowell
Elisha Shepard
Lieut. Frederick Smith
Joseph Smith
Benjamin Tucker
Capt. Phineas Walker
Joel White
Capt. Guy Young

SUDBURY.

Abner Hall
Noah Merritt
Stephen Murray
Peter Reynolds
Serg't Adam Stevens
Asahel Williams

SUNDERLAND.

Capt. Thomas Comstock
Simeon Hicks

STRATTON.

Abel Grout
Bissell Grout
Bille Mann

Samuel Marble
Jonathan Marsh

SUTTON.

Jesse Ainger
Rev. Amos Beckwith
Moses H. Brewer
James Campbell
Serg't Samuel Winslow

SWANTON.

Azariah Brooks
Eleazer Brooks
Hananiah Brooks
Josiah Brush
John B. Joyal
Samuel Todd

THETFORD.

Asa Bond
Serg't Joseph Bruce
Jonathan Child
Richmond Crandall
Robert Farris
John Frizzell
Simon Gillett
Josiah Hubbard
Edward S. Meeder
Levi Parker
Samuel Shepherd
Solomon Strong
James Tyler
Jeremiah Tyler
Richard Wallace

TINMOUTH.

Charles Brewster
Lieut. Nathaniel Chipman
Neri Cramton
Dr. Ebenezer Marvin
Samuel Mattocks
Samuel Noble
Pelatiah Phillips
Beulah Waldo

TOPSHAM.

Adam Dickey
Jacob Wilds

TOWNSHEND.

John Burt
Maj. Samuel Fletcher
Josiah Fisk
Jonas Galusha
Philip Kingsbury
Ebenezer McIvaine
Nathaniel Oaks
Joseph Tyler

TROY.

Moses Hunt
Abner Smith

TUNBRIDGE.

Solomon Cushman
Timothy Dewey
Capt. Benjamin Durkee
Joel Emery
John Hopkins
Hezekiah Hutchinson
John Riddall
Cyrus Tracy
Serg't Elijah Tracy
Peter Whitney

UNDERHILL.

David Berge
Chauncey Graves
George Olds
Caleb Sheldon
Barnard Ward
Oliver Wells

VERGENNES.

Enoch Woodbridge
Phineas Brown

VERNON.

John Dresser
John Fairman
Sylvanus Harris
Isaac Johnson
Stephen Johnson
Jacob Lawton
David Lee
Andrew Parsons

John J. Peeler
Isaac Pratt
Ebenezer Scott
Thomas Sweetland
Jerijah Thayer

VERSHIRE.

Enoch Catlin
Lyman Child
Jesse Paine
Nathan Pierce
Samuel Southworth

WAITSFIELD.

David Bashnell
Gaas Hitchcock
Beriah Sherman
Benjamin Wait

WALDEN.

Serg't Joshua Corson

WALLINGFORD.

James Culver
William Fox
Lieut. Abraham Ives
Lieut. Joseph Randall

WARDSBORO.

Robert Babcock
Thomas Boyle
Gideon Brimhall
Nathaniel Chamberlin
Elisha Converse
Hinsdale Hammond
David Harris
Adam Howard
Samuel Kenney
Daniel Read
Ephraim Rice
John Stacy
Stephen Warren
Edward Walker
Asa Wheelock

WARREN.

John Greenslit
William Porter

Moses Sargent
Richard Shaw
Ruel Sherman

WALTHAM.

Pliny Stannard

WASHINGTON.

Enoch Cheney
Horatio Hobart
Joseph Kenison
Shubel Smith
Thaddeus White

WELLS.

Peter Blossom
William Hart
Robert Hotchkiss
Phineas Lamb
Timothy Moses
Elijah Parks

WATERBURY.

Asaph Allen
John Atkins
Paul Dillingham
Levi Gleason
Roswell Hunt
John Hutson
Cephas Sheldon

WEATHERSFIELD.

Isaac Proctor

WEST FAIRLEE.

William Cox
Solomon Dickinson
Joseph Foster
John Gould
Jonathan Lougee
Stephen May
Calvin Morse
Francis Whitcomb

WESTFORD.

Jesse Atwood
William Chadwick

George Chase
Gideon Dixon
Samuel French
Solomon Hobart
Simeon Hooker
John Lawrence
Serg't John Macomber
Samuel Moore
George Northway
Capt. James Taylor
George Thrasher
Benjamin Wilmont
Josiah Woodruff

WEST HAVEN.

Elijah Tryon

WESTON.

Samuel Martin
John Wait

WESTMINSTER.

Jabez Arms
Sergt. Seth Arnold
Thomas Baldwin
Aaron Bixby
Nathaniel Bixby
Elisha Berry
Stephen R. Bradley
Capt. Jesse Burk
Bysewell Beckwith
James Crawford
William Cronk
Lieut. Nathaniel Doubleday
Isaiah Eaton
Richard Fairbrother
William French
Bartholomew Fuller
Benjamin Goodridge
Benjamin Goodridge, Jr.
Seth Gould
Lot Hall
Aaron Hitchcock
Heli Hitchcock
Charles Holden
Francis Holden
Daniel Houghton
David Houghton

41

Jonathan Houghton
Benjamin Howard
Robert Miller
Henry P. Ranney
Ephraim Ranney
Mark Richards
Reuben Robinson
Benjamin Smith
Benjamin Stone
Linds Tower
Josiah Victor
David Wells
Azariah Wright
Caleb Wright
Thomas Wright

WEST WINDSOR.

Reuben Kendall, Jr.

WHEELOCK.

Ebenezer Chandler

WHITING.

Maj. Samuel Beach
Serg't Noah Bliss
Francis Donita
Ezra Kelsey
Milton Potter
Gideon Walker
Elijah White

WHITINGHAM.

Josiah Brown
Jonathan Cooley
Silas Stickney
Jonathan Tainter

WILLIAMSTOWN.

Edmund Bacon
James Buell
Ephraim Capron
Abijah Clark
Eliphalet Colman
Joseph Crane
Penuel Denning
Joshua Gilman
William Harrington
Moses Jeffords
Henry Johnson
James Kilburn

Cornelius Lynde
Elijah Paine
Shubael Simons
James Smith
John Smith
Sylvester Smith
Timothy Snow
Job Thompson

WILLISTON.

Elisha Bradley
Joseph Bradley
Robert Beach
Dr. Thomas Binney
Serg't John Brown
Thomas Chittenden
Paul Clark
Joseph Edmonds
Thaddeus Graves
Col. Isaac McNeil
Solomon Miller

WILMINGTON.

Asher Alvord
Serg't Adnah Bangs
Caleb Baldwin
Jedediah Bassett
Charles Bellows
Abraham Boyd
Abram Boyd
Robert Boyd
Samuel Bridge
John Buck
Moses Buck
Samuel Buell
Roger Burchard
Timothy Castle
Simeon Chandler
Jonathan Childs
Jesse Cook
Joseph Cook
Robert Cook
Daniel Cutting
Daniel Dickenson
Ozias Dix
Warren Eastbrook
Elijah Easton
Jesse Fitch
John Fitch
Stephen Forbes

James Flagg
Josiah Flagg
Stephen Foster
Theophilus Foster
Nathan Fox
Watson Freeman
John Gibbs
Andrew Haskell
Thomas Haskell
William Haskell
Jonathan Hastings
Asa Havens
Abraham Haynes
Serg't Jonas Haynes
Reuben Haynes
David Jillson
Jonathan Johnson
Jonathan Lamb
Serg't Israel Lawton
Jonah Lincoln
Daniel Livermore
John Marks
Benjamin Metcalf
Isaac Miller
Judah Moore
Reuben Morgan
Jesse Mossman
Samuel Murdock
Joseph Nye
Levi Packard
Jeremiah Parmelee
James Smith
Medad Smith
Daniel Stearns
Josiah Stearns
Reuben Stearns
Jesse Swift
Samuel Thompson
Ephraim Titus
Jeremiah Wheeler
Barni Wing
Jonathan Witt

WINDHAM.

Samuel Ayers
Jonathan Britnall
John Burnap
John Cole
Stephen Fitch
Archibald Mack

John Mack
Archibald McCormic
Nehemiah Peirce
Daniel Putnam

WINDSOR.

Sewall Blood
Benjamin Cole
Stephen Conant
Walter Gilkey
Samuel Hutchinson
Samuel Marcy
Jereboam Swain
Capt. Benjamin Skinner
Andrew Stevens
Capt. Moses White

WINHALL.

John Brooks

WOLCOTT.

Seth Hubbell

WOODBURY.

Joseph Blanchard
David Rugg
Comfort Wheeler

WOODSTOCK.

James Bishop
Lieut. Abner Brigham
Jesse Bruce
Rufus Carpenter
John Darling
John Doton
James Fletcher
Daniel Fraser
Lieut. Nathan Howland
Jabez King
Andrew McWaine
Joel Perkins
Phineas Raymond
Lieut. Israel Richardson
Amaziah Richmond
Nathaniel Ruggles
Phinehas Sanderson
Benjamin Thompson
Jacob Wilder

WORCESTER.

Stephen Spear

INVALID PENSIONERS.

ADDISON COUNTY.

David Barber
Peter Bradley
Calvin Bingham
Jacob Chase
Jason Eager
Bethuel Goodrich, Jr.
Martin Hatch
Sergt. Henry Jones, 2nd
Henry Jones
Russell Jefferson
William Jourdon
William Kellogg
Serg't Adam Muir
Levi Plumbley
Thomas Stevens
Serg't Calvin Stewart
Abraham Vandenberg
Henry Wilson
Joseph Walbridge

BENNINGTON COUNTY.

Ephraim Bowen
Serg't James A. Bennett
Benjamin Grover
Nathan B. Harvey
Zenas Jones
George W. King
Jonathan Lyon
John Talman
Richard C. Wear

CALEDONIA COUNTY.

Hastings Blanchard
James Chesley
Eben Fisk
Judson Farrah·
Wells Goodwin
Samuel Haviland
Joseph Hackett
Augustus Monroe

CHITTENDEN COUNTY.

Lyman Allen
Jonathan Allen

Alanson Adams
Reuben Butler
Serg't Joseph H. Bryant
Daniel Bennett
Guy Beebee
Benjamin Butcher
Robert Cockle
James Gatchell
Zebulon Gilman
Arthur Hogan
Asa Hull
William Humphrey
Harvey Johnston
David Lathe
John McLeod
Lawrence Pano
Sergt. Levi Pratt
Lieut. Frederick A. Sawyer
John Titus
Peter Wilhelm
John Williams

ESSEX COUNTY.

Adam Bartlett
Jonathan Hoyt

FRANKLIN COUNTY.

James Austin
Alfred Eldredge
Serg't Gardner Foster
Artiban Hoit
Uriah Higgins
John Newton
Justus Powers
Lemuel Scott
Alpheus Smith, Jr.
Obed Snow
Harry Sykes
Frederick Wilkins

GRAND ISLÉ COUNTY.

Charles Cortwite
Eleazer Martin
Thomas Reynolds
Abraham Woodard

44

ORANGE COUNTY.

Solomon Clark
Charles Collins
Lieut. John W. Cushing
John Darling
Experians Fisk, Jr.
Manzel Hazelton
James Mellen
Ebenezer Smith
Nicholas C. Wells

ORLEANS COUNTY.

Stephen Barnard
John Bickford
John Collins
Joshua Foss
Serg't Frederick Fuller
Joshua Gilman
Gideon Griggs
John Hadley
Jonas Harrington
Ela Haynes (or Hinds)
Stephen F. Hemingway
Nathaniel Hewett
Nathaniel Norris
Adam Sumner
Walter Waller

RUTLAND COUNTY.

Stephen Angervine
John Bell
Serg't Elial Bond
Lieut. Daniel Farrington
Nathan Ford
Solomon Gibbs
Moses Head
John Herrick
Roswell Hunt
Thomas Mitchell
Charles Obriham
Rufus Parker
Elnathan Phelps
Ira Remington
Prince Robinson
Elnathan Ward

David Warren
Abel Woods

WASHINGTON COUNTY.

Isaac Billings
Laban Brown
Richard Buchanan
James Green
James Harvey
Jason March
Adonijah B. Rogers

WINDHAM COUNTY.

Oliver Darling
Isaac Gleason
William Hazeltine
Thomas Lowe
Calvin P. Perry
Serg't Daniel Reed
Elihu Sabin
Chauncey L. Temple

WINDSOR COUNTY.

Daniel Averill
Serg't Alfred Barrel
Ezra Bellows
Daniel Boynton
Aden Bullard
Serg't Giles Cone
Ezekiel Cook
Capt. David Crawford
Calvin Dike
Serg't Andrew Dunlap
William Fisk
Serg't Charles French
John M. Goodrich
Calvin Green
Zera Green
Willard Huntoon
John Morgan
Alba Southard
James Stevens
Amasa Turner
Robert White

LIST OF INVALID PENSIONERS WHO RECEIVED PENSIONS AT THÉ BUR-
LINGTON AGENCY, BUT WHOSE RESIDENCE COULD NOT BÉ ASCER-
TAINÉD, OWING TO THE DESTRUCTION OF PAPERS IN THE WAR
OFFICE IN 1801 AND 1814.

Jonas Adams
Elijah Barnes
Samuel Bradish
Daniel Brown
Thomas Brush
Elisha Capron
Frederick Carter
Gershom Clark
Samuel Eyres
Ezra Gates
Thomas Green
Jonathan Haynes
Jared Hinkley
William Hunt
Charles Huntoon
Lieut. Joseph Huntoon
Serg't Seth Ingram
Joseph B. Lovewell
Abraham Merryfield

Richard Millen
Lieut. Elnathan Nichols
Col. John Nixon
Elisha Norton
Pliney (Pliny) Pomeroy
Jonathan Preston
Nehemiah Price
Peter Rider
John Roberts
Amasa Scott
Ephraim Smith
Capt. John Stark
Uriah Stone
Joseph Tyler
Horace B. Thompson
Aaron Wilder
Ephraim Wilmarth
Serg't John Wilson
William Woodruff

PENSIONERS UNDER THE ACT OF MARCH 18, 1818.

ADDISON COUNTY.

Solomon Aiken
John Alexander
Ezra Allen
Heman Amy
Benjamin Andrews
Samuel Andrews
Lieut. Samuel Bache
Capt. John Bacon
Isaac Barrows
Jonathan Belding
Simeon Blanchard
Leeman Brownson
David Brydia
Daniel Ball
Asahel Beebe
Solomon Beebe
Jesse Bishop
Elijah Branch
Edward Calley (or Kelley)
Timothy Case
Henry Chamberlin
Leander Chamberlin

Swift Chamberlin
Peter Chartier
Capt. Peter Clayes
David Clough
Sergt. Anthony Collamore
Asa Crane
John Crane
Zachariah Curtis
Nathaniel Cushman
Levi Darling
Peter Davis
John C. Despervine (or Taper-
vine)
John Dibble
Daniel Dike
John Downing
Elisha Dunham
Luther Eaton
Jonathan Eldridge
James Farmer
Edward Forbes
Calvin Goodno
Nathan Griffith
Edmund Grundy

John Hodgdon
Benjamin Hodge
Ephraim Holdridge
Serg't Jonathan Hunter
Nathan Jaques
Prince Jenney
Nathaniel Joy
Solomon Kellogg
William Kilbourn
James Lawrence
George Leonard
Lemuel Luddington
Thomas N. Martin
Philip McKenzie
Jacob McLean
Serg't Thomas McNeill
Benjamin Mead
Ely Nichols
David Page
Ebenezer Palmer
Stephen Parker
Joseph Payne
Benjamin Plumley
Jonathan Plumley
Paul Pond
Joseph Powers
Owen Records
Richard Shaw
William Spooner
Nathan Sprague
Samuel Sunderland
Samuel Taylor
Stephen Terrill
Jonathan Treadway
Samuel Walker
Michael Welsh
Samuel Wetherell
Moses Wheeler
Joshua Whitney
Abner Wilcox
Timothy Woodward

BENNINGTON COUNTY.

Oliver Alden
Adam Amsden
Jesse Banister
Thomas Banister
Francis Bates
Joseph Beaman
Selah B. Benjamin

Stephen Bennett, 2nd
Abner Blackmar
William Blasdell
Ephraim Blowers
Cornelius Bracy
Abijah Brown
Hezekiah Carey
Ebenezer Chace
Samuel Church
Ward Clark
Shubael Cook
John Corkins
John Crafford
William Cummings
Josiah Cutler
Gideon Davis
James Davis
Joseph Day
Benedict Eggleston
Daniel Evans
George Fields
Joseph Freeman
Jotham French
Benjamin Glazier
George Goby
George Godfry
Allen Graves
David Gray
William Harris, 2nd
Benoni Hawkins
John Holly
Elisha Houghton
Joseph House
Joseph Howe
David Jepson
Titus Kellogg
Ezra Keys
Jabez Knap
Benjamin Lamb
Ebenezer Lillie
Elisha Lincoln
Asahel Lucas
John Marble
Jacob Martin
Stephen Merrill
Gideon Myers
Seth Pollard
Silas Pratt
William Pratt
Humphrey Richardson
George Robinson

David Sawyer
Joseph Smith, 2nd
Samuel Stacey
Serg't Nathaniel Thompson
Ebenezer Temple
Oliver Tidd
Asa Thatcher
Samuel Thayer
Simeon Thayer
Sergt. Nathaniel Thompson
Ebenezer Upham
Edward Wade
Henry Wakelin
Daniel Welsh
John Welsh
Nathan Whipple
David White
John Wiley
John Wiman
Charles Winchester

CALEDONIA COUNTY.

John Allen
Josiah Bachelder
James Ball
Nathan Barker
Henry Blake
Joseph Blanchard
Nathaniel Burbank
Wells Burbank
Zebulon Burroughs
James Campbell, 2nd
John Chaplin
Edward Clark
Joseph Conner
Moses Darling
Nathan Edson
Moses Evans
Eben Farman
Manassah Farnsworth
John Fox
Serg't Thomas Fuller
Paul Gale
Nathaniel Glines
Alvin Goodall
Silas Gorham
Elias Hall
Pearly Harris
Archibald Harvey
Thomas Haseltine

Starling Heath
John Jenness
William Johnston
John Kelley
Joab Kimball
Edward Magoon
Eleazer Nutting
Sergt. William Orcutt
Thomas Osgood
Foster Page
Nehemiah Philips
Edward Pollard
Daniel Quinley
John Rollins
David Rugg
Ebenezer Sawyer
Bela Shaw
Caleb Stiles
Stephen Sweetser
William Trescott
Serg't Paul Wells

CHITTENDEN COUNTY.

Alexander Alford
Robert Averill
Daniel Barnum
Friend Beeman
Lieut. Peter Benedict
William Bliss
Serg't Joseph Bonett
Samuel Burns
Isaac Bump
Benjamin Butcher, 2nd
Samuel Chase
John Cobb
Samuel Collamer
Ebenezer Cook
Jared Dixon
Alexander Durand
Serg't Thomas Eddy
Ebenezer Flagg
Ebenezer Fox
Lemuel French
Samuel Fuller
Serg't Samuel Hill
Samuel Hinkson
Lieut. John Hollenback (or Hollomback)
Daniel Howe
Augustus Lavoke (or Lavoque)

John Lawrence
John Martin
James Morey
Caleb Nash
Andrew Neal
Thomas Newman
Prince Peters
Aaron Potter
Amos Preston
Reuben Ray
Isaac Rexford
Asa Rider
Freelove Roberts
Robert Rollins
Nathan Seymour
Jabez Spicer
Roger Stevens
Lieut. Safford Stevens
William Straw
Eliphalet Tomlinson
Simon Tubbs
Serg't Hezekiah Tuttle
Jonathan Wood
Thomas Woodward

ESSEX COUNTY.

Josiah Abbott
Elijah Blodgett
Gershom Boston
Samuel Clay
Chancey Curtis
Ezekiel Flanders
David Hagar
Charles Hanson
James Luther
Samuel Martin
Nathaniel Moulton
Mansfield Nichols
Jeremiah Parmelee
Hinds Reed
Silas Simonds
Benjamin Streeter
Samuel Turner
Noah Villas
Robert Wallis
Lot Woodbury

FRANKLIN COUNTY.

Philip Alexander
John Andrus

Thomas Atwood
Benjamin Barnet
Enoch Beals
Foard Bears
Isaac Billings
Silas Billings
Joseph Bowdish
Jeffrey Brace (alias J. Stiles)
Jude Brown
John Burlinson
Isaac Butler
Abraham Carman
Roswell Catlin
Comfort Chaffer
Ebenezer Chamberlain
Aaron Chase
Reuben Craw
Jonathan Danforth
John Delaway
Jonathan Farnsworth
Simeon Foster
Jacob Garland
Sergt. David George
Michael George
David Gibbs
Obadiah Gilbert
Joshua Goodridge
George Gragg
Lieut. Benoni Grant
Isaac Gregg
Benjamin Griswold
William Heath
Jehiel Holdridge
Jehiel Hull
Wait Hurlbut
William Jeffords
Serg't Benjamin Joy
Micah Joy
William Kelly, 2nd
Thomas Keyes
Eleazer Knapp
Isaac Lackey
Samuel Laflin
Joseph Lamb
Theophilus Larrabee
John Lawrence, 2nd
Benjamin Leach
John McNamara
Silas McWithey
James Miller
Serg't Samuel Mitchell

Timothy Mitchell
Tho. Nash (alias Hunter)
Samuel Niles
Elijah Nutting
John Nutting
Aaron Olds
John Otis
Ansel Patterson
Ebenezer Pease
Joel W. Perham
Daniel Perkins
Daniel Perkins, 2nd
David Perrigo
Putnam Phelps
James Pierce
Elijah Pratt
William Prior
Joseph Randall
Robert Rummells
William Sanders
Jacob Seagel
George Shepard
Jedediah Sherwood
Isaac Smith, 2nd
Ithamer Smith
Nathan Smith
Ebenezer Stebbins
Francis Stewart
Isaac Tillotson
Nathaniel B. Torrey
Serg't Stephen Trowbridge
Benjamin Welch
Ephraim Whitcomb
David White
Jared Wilcox
Asa Wilkins
Lieut. Josiah Witter
Gideon Wood
Robert Wood
Roger Woodworth
Jehiel Wright

GRAND ISLE COUNTY.

John Bean
Benjamin Bell
Joseph Butler
William Cady
Josiah Knight
William McAllister
Cloud Monty
Stephen Paine

ORANGE COUNTY.

Timothy Abbott
Samuel Adams
Amos Allen
James Andrews
Michael Archer
John Barnes
Edward Bass
Moses Bates
Rosiah Beedy
John Blackmore
Lieut. Thomas Bingham
James Bishop
William Boardman
Thomas Bogle
Ananiah Bohonon
John Proctor Borres
Enoch Bowen
Charles Bowles
Moses Bragg
Abraham Brigham
Capt. Paul Brigham
Eleazer Brown
Benjamin Burgess
John Burk
Jonathan Cadwell
Sergt. Richard Carlton
Lieut. John Chadwick
Joseph Chamberlain
Lieut. Isaac Church
Jonathan Churchill
Daniel Cilley
Reuben Clement
Salem Colbey
Edward Cowdery
Samuel Corless
Timothy Corless
Nero Cross
John Cummings
Simeon Curtis
Obadiah Davis
Gideon Dickinson
Jonathan Downing
Ebenezer Drake
Ichabod Dyer
Josiah Eastman
Qm. Sergt. Samuel Edson
John Fellows
Jacob Flanders
Nathaniel Flint

John Findly
Samuel Freeman
Joshua Geary
Moses S. George
Simon Gillet
Irijah Green
Amasa Grover
Nathan Haines
James Havens
Joseph Hixon
Samuel Houghton
Enoch Hoyt
Daniel Hunt
Charles Hunton
Elisha Hutchinson
Stephen Jenkins
Serg't John Keyes
William Kincade
Richard Kimball
Thomas Kinney
George Knox
Thomas Lancaster
Levi Lawrence
Nathaniel Leeds
Alexander Leslie
John Lines
Samuel Linsey
Levi Lufkin
Benjamin Mack
John Martin
Thomas May
Samuel McKellups
Thomas McKirth
Benoni Morey
Joseph Orn
Nathan Page
Thomas Parker
Moses Pearson
Sergt. Samuel Peck
Daniel Philbrick
Mathew Pratt
Benjamin Preston
John Putnam
John Rand
Samuel Randall
Lieut. Joseph Raymond
Jonathan Read
John Rice
Merrick Rice
Richard Rindge
Ephraim Rollf

James Rowell
Moses Rowell
Lieut. Cornelius Russell
Conant Sawyer
Isaac Skinner
Benjamin Smith
John Smith, 3rd
Jedediah Smith
Zachariah Smith
Lemuel Southworth
Ebenezer Stacey
Serg't John Stacey
John Stewart
Francis Thompson
George Townsend
John Underwood
Lieut. Joseph Wales
Charles Weed
John Welch
Daniel Wentworth
Jabez Wight
George Williamson
Jonathan Wills
Ebenezer Wood
Daniel Woods
Peter Youngman
Thomas Youngman

ORLEANS COUNTY.

Elias Bingham
Ebenezer Broughton
Isaac Clement
John Cole
Paul Cook
Nathan Cross
Daniel Davison
Qm. Serg't Seth Eddy
Isaac Fletcher
William Hamblett
Benjamin Hardy
James Harlow
John Healy
Lieut. Jonathan Heath
Timothy Hinman
Serg't David Hopkinson
Moses Hunt
Humphrey Nichols
Jonathan Norris
Moses Norris
John Palmer
Simeon Pope

Joel Priest
Serg't William Richardson
David Ripley
Josiah Roberts
William Sisco
Ephraim Skinner
Joseph Slack
Benjamin Stebbins
Jonathan Taylor
Loring Thompson
Lieut. Thomas Tolman
Samuel Turner, 2nd
John Vance
Benjamin Varnum
Edward Welch
Archipus Wheelock
Peter Wylie

RUTLAND COUNTY.

Joshua Adams
Eliakim Aikin
Eleazer (or John) Albee
Zebulon Ames
Samuel Ayres
Timothy Backus
Jonathan Bagley
Peter Baker
Josiah Baldwin
John Banker
Ithiel Barnes
Alexander Barr
Ezekiel Beebe
Brister Bennet
Jonas Bennet
Seth Benson
Benjamin Blossom
Isaac Bowen
Daniel Burlingame
Roger Burr
Eli Calkin
Lemuel Chapman
Benjamin Chamberlain
Solomon Chittenden
Asa Clark
Oren Clark
Solomon Collins
Thomas Collins
William Cook
David Cross
John Daniels

Barnabas Davidson
John Davis
Douglas Davison
Ebenezer Dearst
Jerathmiel Doty
Jesse Doud
Samuel Drew
Caleb Eddy
Jonathan Fletcher
Abel Foster
Joseph Frost
Capt. John Fuller
Seth Gansey
Cornelius Gibbs
Thomas Gibbs 2nd
Ebenezer Gibs
William Gill
Elijah Goodwin
Jacob Gould
Daniel Hardy
Jacob Hibbard
Serg't Samuel Hill
Isaac Hoisington
John Howe
Joseph Howland
Jonas Hubbard
Selah Hubbard
William Hunt
Serg't Thomas Hutchinson
Jonathan Jackson
Isaiah Jacobs
Timothy Johnson
Aaron Keeler
Amos Kimball
Jedediah Kimball
Amos Lawrence
Moses Leach
James Ledget
Simeon Leonard
Daniel Lincoln
John Lynch
James Martin
John May
Christopher Miner
Ichabod Mitchell
John Moors
Abraham Moses
Revivius Newell
Daniel Newton
Eliada Orton
Nathan Osgood

Joseph Owen
John Page
Benjamin Palmeton
Barzilla Phillips
James Phillips
John Phillips
Joseph M. Pine
Zebulon Pond
Peter Powers
Lemuel Pratt
John Priest
Samuel Priest
Timothy Prince
Joshua Randall
Samuel Ranger
Gilbert Ray
Luke Roberts
Simeon Russell 2nd
Sergt. John Sallings
Isaac Saunders
Jacob Sawyer
Zadock Scribner
Henry Sellick
Jedediah Seward
David Shays
Jonathan Sheppard
Dan Smith
John Smith 2nd
Jonathan Smith
Roger Smith
Timothy Smith
William Smith
Prince Soper
Ephraim Stephens
Serg't John Sweetland
Edward Taylor
Jacob Thayer
William Thomas
Samuel Torrey
Serg't Solomon Tracy
Abial Trafton
Moses Turner
Qm. Serg't Jabez Ward
Badwell Watkins
Jesse Watson
Elijah Wentworth
Jonathan Williams
Thomas Williams
Henry Wilson
Joshua Wood
Josiah Wood

WASHINGTON COUNTY.

Benjamin Alden
George Allen
Carver Bates
Ebenezer Bean
Joseph Bennett
Parrit Blasdell
Asa Boutwell
Thomas Carr 2nd
Moses Chase
Timothy Claflin
Aaron Clough
Caleb Cotton
Samuel Currier
John Davidson
Jonathan Davis
Samuel Davis
Jonathan Delano
Benjamin Dix
Nathaniel B. Dodge
Archelaus Dwinel
Elisha Goodspeed
Azariah Grant
Joseph Hamilton
Estes Hatch
Joseph Hobart
John Hudson
David Johnson
Thomas Jones
Giles Kelsey
William Kenney
James Kilborn
James Latham
Richard Lyman
David Mack
George Martin 2nd
Obadiah Morse
Moses Nelson
Apollos Paddock
Noah Pearson
Asa Poland
Moses Rood
Asa Richardson
Abel Sawyer
David Sloan
Timothy Snow
Primus Story
Elias Taylor
Lieut. David Thomas
Thomas Thompson

Ephraim Town
David Town
David V. Town
John Vinton
Joshua Wade
Jeduthun Wait
Josiah Wright 2nd

WINDHAM COUNTY.

Philip Adams
Isaac Armsden
Thomas Atcherson
George Austin
Samuel Bailey
Jeremiah Barrett
Sergt. Edmund Bemis
Barzilla Benjamin
Thomas Betterley
Solomon Blodget
Timothy Bolton
Isaiah Booth
John Bradley
Gideon Briggs
Jacob Brown
Serg't Silas Brown
Jonathan Burk
John Burnham
Ebenezer Chamberlain
Stephen Chase
Joseph Cleaveland
Eleazer Cobleigh
Nathaniel Cole
Ezekiel Cook
Josiah Cutler
Nathaniel Cutler
John Darling
Benjamin Davis
Henry Davis
John L. Davis
Amos Dennison
Peter Derry
Jonathan Dix
John Dudley
Abijah Eaton
Jonathan Emmons
Asa Fay
John Firnham
Timothy Fisher
Thomas French
Gamaliel Gerald

Thomas Gleason
Jacob Gilson
Solomon Gilson
Andrew Grimes
Thomas Harris
Ichabod Higgins
Asahel Hill
John Hogan
Amos Holbrook
Richard Hunt
James Huzzey
Ephraim Jackson
Robert Jenison
Benjamin Jewell
Grindell Keith
Peter Lamb
Jacob Laughton
Samuel Lovering
Thomas Low
Jonathan Marble, Jr.
Jason Makepeace
Serg't Jesse Marks
James Mayar
Sylvester Mattoon
William Miner
Samuel Moore
Samuel Newton
Miller Paine
Ezekiel Perham
Lieut. Joseph Perry
John Priest
Amos Puffer
Stephan Putnam
Bailey Rawson
Thomas Reed 2nd
John Roberts
John Rozier
Capt. Amasa Soper
Jonathan Stearns
William Steward
William Stoodley
Joseph Swain
Abraham Tuttle
Joseph Underwood
Elijah Wallsworth
Calvin Weld
John Welman
Hezekiah Wetherbee
Eleazer Whitney
Timothy Wilcox
John Williams 2nd

Nathaniel Wooley
Asa Miller Wyman
Uzziah Wyman

WINDSOR COUNTY.

Isaac Adams
Jonas Adams
Sergt. Levi Adams
Samuel G. Allen
John Atherton
Joshua Austin
Samuel Avery
Joel Babbit
Elijah Backus
Hart Balch
Humphrey Ball
Hananiah Barker
Oliver Barrett
Howard Bassett
Zachariah Bassett
Josiah Bates
Ebenezer Billings
Adonijah Bixby
William Brown 2nd
Solomon Briggs
Serg't Jonas Bruce
Benjamin Bugbee
Zadock Barnum
David Burton
James Byram
Robert Campbell
Lieut. Ephraim Carey
Jedediah Caswell
Sylvanus Chadwick
David Chaffin
Samuel Chase
Stephen Child
Joshua Church
Ephraim Claflin
Sergt. Samuel Clapp
Ebenezer Clark
Paul Clark
Waters Clark
Julius Colton
Serg't William Cone
Humphrey Crain
Ebenezer Currier 2nd.
Jonas Cutting
Josiah Dana
Nathan Davis

Joseph Demick
Shadrack Dodge
Charles Dorothy
Joseph Doubleday
Robert Dunbar
Ephraim Dutton
David Earle
Samuel Ellinwood
Oliver Fairbanks
Ebenezer Farnsworth
Joseph Farnsworth
Francis Faxon
Moses Fay
Thomas Fay
Nathan Fellows
Samuel Finney
Robert Forrest
Jonathan Foster
Prince Freeman
Jonathan French
Willard Frink
James Gaines
John Gibson
John Gill
Serg't Aaron Glazier
Isaac Glinney
John Goodrich
Benjamin Green
Isaac Green
Ephraim Griggs
Jacob Grover
Recompence Hall
Simeon Harrington
Seth Hart
Ichabod Hatch
David Hesselton
Richard Hill
Nathaniel Hitchcock
Serg't Elkanah Hixon
Thomas Hoadley
Benjamin Hoit
Abraham Holden
Joseph Holden
Reuben Holland
William Holt
Capt. John House
Simon Howe
Serg't Maj. Abner Hubbard
Samuel Hutchinson 2nd
Stephen Jennings
Jedediah Jepherson

William Jewell
James Johnson
Uriah Johnson
William Kirk
Daniel Knight
John Knowze
William Labaron
Jonathan Lake
Shubael Lanphere
Nicholas Lawrence
Enoch Learned
Lieut. Benjamin Lynde
Edward Lyon
John Mallard
Daniel Marsh
Christopher Martin
Sergt. Ephraim Martin
George Martin
Reuben McCollister
John Moor Jr.
John Moore
Alexander Murray
Lieut. Samuel Myrick
Jonathan Newman
Samuel Newton 2nd
John Nichols
Elijah Norton
Sergt. Benjamin Packard
Moses Page
Charles Pain
Ezekiel Palmer
Jonah Palmer
Philemon Parker
Silas Parker
John Patrick
Joseph Pease
Benjamin Peirce 2nd
David Peirce
Joseph Perham
Abner Perry
Daniel Perry
Silas Perry
Joshua Phillips
Asahel Powers
Robert Preston
Samuel Proctor
Elnathan Reed
Jonathan Reynolds
Isaac Rice
Lemuel Richards

Ezra Ritter
John Robbins
Rufus Root
John Row
Caesar Sankee
Jonathan Sawyer
John Scott
Abbe Severance
Sylvanus Shaw
Francis Sinclair
William Slack
Nathaniel Smith
Peter Smith
Samuel Smith
Caleb Snow
Jonathan Snow
Joshua Spear
Benjamin Spooner
Charles Spooner
Lincoln Stiles
Phineas Strong
Artemas Taft
Frederick Temple
Benjamin Tenny
John O. Thacher
Joseph Tucker
Nathaniel Tufts
James Upham
Elisha Ward
Nathan Watkins
Thomas Weatherbee
Thomas Weeden
Sergt. Asa Wneeler
Jonathan Wheelock
Sergt. Jotham Wheelock
Archibald White
Francis White
Benjamin Whitmore
Abner Whitney
John Whitly
Levi Wilder
James Willis
Caleb Williston
David Wiswell
Eleazer Wood
Ebenezer Woodward
Nehemiah Woodward
Timothy Woodworth
Clark Young

PENSIONERS UNDER THE ACT OF JUNE 7, 1832.

ADDISON COUNTY.

Lieut. Samuel Adams
Lieut. James Andrews
Sergt Ethan Andrus
Nathaniel Austin
Sergt. James Barber
Rufus Barnard
Ruppe Batchelder
Calvin Bliss
Joseph Bird
Benjamin Bissell
Alpheus Brooks
Nathan Brown
Sergt. Solomon Brown
Jonathan Burnam
Doud Bushnell
Solomon Carter
Jirch Chamberlain
Daniel Champin
Lemuel Chase
Ezra Chilson
Josiah Clark
William Cook
James Crane
Eliakim Culver
Martin Curtis
Samuel Darrow
Moses Dow
Thomas Dudley
Abram Dunning
Ezra Evarts
Eliphalet Farnam
Frederick Frost
Reuben Gillet
Adam Gillmore
Eben Goodenow
Abner Hall
Gershom Hall
Samuel Hall
John Halsey
Daniel Hamblin
John Hamblin
Levi Hanks
Abraham Holden
Solomon Howe
Nathan Hoyt
Sergt. Allen Hunsdon

Job Hutchinson
Lewis Jacobs
Noah Jones
Zebulon Jones
Gershom Justin
Elijah Keeler
Stephen King
Eli Lewis
John Looker
Ezra Loomis
Jonathan Marvin
Matthew Mason
Samuel Martin
Philemon Metcalf
Richard Miner
Hebard Morrill
Bezaleel Myrick
Solomon Naughton
Luther Newcomb
Sergt. William Niles
James Palmer
Jacob Peck
Jathleel Peck
Reuben Peck
Dan Pond
Jacob Post
Truman Pratt
Moses Robbins
Jeremiah Rockwell
Jonathan Rowell
Joshua Rugg
James Shaw
William Shepard
Sergt. James Sibley
Benoni Shurtliff
Oliver Smith
Sergt. Roswell Stearns
Asa Strong
Hilyer Tanner
Jesse Thomas
Joseph Torrence
Thomas Vradenburgh
Israel Wadsworth
John C. Waller
Benjamin Whitman
Andrew Wright
William Young

BENNINGTON COUNTY.

Jonathan Aiken
Sylvester Andrew
Asa Andrews
Benjamin Barnard
Elijah Barton
Sergt. Lemuel Bishop
John Blanchard
Benjamin Bowen
James Bowen
John Croswell
Sergt. Joseph Curtis
Elias Demick
Aaron Denis
Obadiah Dunham
Sergt. William Dunton
John Fuller
John Frost
Peter Gould
Abraham Grimes
Reuben Gulliver
James Hamilton
Seth Harmon
Moses Hastings
Seth Hathaway
Israel Hays
Sergt. Isaiah Hendryx
James Hicks
Isaac Hill
Levi Hill
Asahel Hollister
Zaccheus Hovey
Sergt. Aaron Hubbell
John Huling
Adam Hurd
Elijah Hurd
Asa Kinne
Charles Ledyard
Emmons Lillie
Simeon Littlefield
Jesse Loomis
James Merrill
Josiah Montgomery
Edward Moore
Sergt. Grove Moore
Benjamin Morgan
Joseph Myrick
Martin Norton
Zadock Norton
Zacheriah Paddeford

Qm. William Park
Charles Parker
John Parker
Sergt. Eli Pettibone
Stephen Pratt
Elisha Raymond
Sergt. John Risdon
Isaac Roberts
Sergt. Jacob Safford
Solomon Safford
Lieut. Ephraim Seelye
Moses Sheldon
Enoch Sherman
James Sweet
Ashbel Sykes
Joel Taylor
Joseph Thorp
Nathaniel Towsley
James Uran
Solomon Wade
Samuel Wallice
Samuel Walker
Daniel Warner
David Weeks
Ebenezer Welch
Oliver Wellman
Prosper Wheeler
Samuel Wilkinson
William Wiman
Noah Woodward
Solomon Wright

CALEDONIA COUNTY.

Asquire Aldrich
Abner Allen
Uri Babbitt
Jethro Bachelder
Jonathan Badger
Luther Bailey
Sergt. Obadiah Barber
Thomas Beedle
John Bly
Elisha Cate
Daniel Chappel
Samuel Clark
Seth Clark
Zachariah Clifford
Abner Coe
Jedediah Coe
Thomas Colby

Abel Conant
Jonathan Curtis
Sergt. Samuel Daniels
Samuel Davis
Benjamin Deming
Stephen Dexter
Benjamin Dow
Nathaniel Dow
David Durant
Sergt. Benjamin Farmer
Nathaniel Farrington
Abraham Fuller
Jason Fuller
Levi Hall
Thomas Hall
Nathaniel Hayward
James Heath
Samuel Hill
Sergt. Thomas Hill
Sergt. Henry Hoffman
Ebenezer Holbrook
Thomas Hoyt
Moses Huntley
Joseph Knight
William Knox
Jonathan Lewis
Ashbel Martin
David Martin
Sergt. Isaac Martin
James McFarland
Isaac Miner
James Miner
Sergt. Jeremiah Morrill
Joseph Morrill
Ephraim Niles
Lemuel Northrop
Sergt. Gaius Peck
Nathaniel Perkins
Oliver Phelps
Daniel Pike
Thaddeus Potter
Jonathan Powers
Jonathan Randall
Elijah Ross
Theophilus Rundlet
William Sawyer
Jonathan Sheldon
Timothy Shurtleff
Esek Smith
Samuel Spaulding
Ebenezer Spencer

Jonathan Sprague
Allen Stewart
Isaac Stowell
Simeon Walker
John Walter
Sergt. Samuel Warner
Stephen Watkins
Ephraim Wesson
Nathaniel Wheeler
Henry Williams
Sergt. Joseph Wood
Benjamin Wright

CHITTENDEN COUNTY.

Sergt. Abijah Allen
Nathan Allen
Elisha Ashley
Wyman Averill
Moses Barnett
John Beach
Robert Beach
Friend Beeman
Isaac Benham
James Bennett
John Blake
Nathaniel Blood
Eber Bradley
Sergt. Edward Brigham
Benton Buck
Justus Byington
Samuel Calhoun
Isaac Chace
Evans Chance
Benoni Chapin
Ichabod Chapin
Archibald Cook
Solomon Cooley
Levi Comstock
John Cunningham
Sergt. John Curry
Simon Davis
Sergt. John Devereaux
Jarrad Farrand
Joseph Farrand
Nathan Fay
Jeremiah Fisher
John Forbes
Asa Graves
Thadeus Graves
Zachariah Hart

Sergt. Elnathan **Higbe**
Abel Hildreath
Leonard Hodges
Simon Hutchins
Daniel Isham
Jirah Isham
David Lamson
Elon Lee
Elisha Leonard
Moses Leonard
Abierther Lincoln
John Linkon
Elisha Meech
Samuel Mills
Daniel Morse
John Moses
Nathaniel Newell
Elias Nye
Elisha Owens
John Palmer
Samuel Parks
Robert Pennell
Thomas Pierpoint
Daniel Robins
Josiah Sheldon
Jacob Snider
Daniel Stearns
Eliphaz Steele
Jesse Stockwell
James Taylor
Thomas Tousley
Jabez J. Warner
David Webster
Joseph Willcox

ESSEX COUNTY.

Sergt. Edward Adams
Joseph Ball
Orsamas Bailey
Joseph Booty
Nathan Bucher
Gilman Clough
Mills De Forrest
Samuel Howe
John Hughs
John Melendy
Sergt. John Merrill
Sergt. Jacob Schoff
Amos Underwood

FRANKLIN COUNTY.

Lieut. Joseph Andrews
Jeremiah Austin
John Austin
John Badger
Whitmore Beardsley
Asahel Berry
Reuben Bruce
Zebulon Buker
Eliphalet Carpenter
William Castor
Daniel Chandler
Oliver Collier
Henry Collins
Luther Cooley
Abel Davis
Cornelius Davis
Kitteridge Davis
Arthur Dorrah
Ralph Ellenwood
Reuben Evarts
Abel Fairbanks
Jonathan Farnsworth
James Fisk
Asa Fleming
Ezekiel Fullington
Francis Goodridge
Elihu Grout
Erastus Hathaway
John Hayward
Joseph Herriman
James Hill
Uri Hill
Sergt. Luke Hitchcock
Jonas Houghton
Nathan Hoyt
John Hunkins
Ephraim Jewel
Jonah Johnson
Israel Jones
Philip Ingram
Ruel Keith
Unite Keith
Asa Ladd
Edmund Lamb
Richard Lattin
Jonathan Mahurin
Samuel Miller
Rufus Montague

David Packard
Amos Page
Parker Page
Thomas Page
Sergt. Josiah Peckham
Rufus Perrigo
Amos Philips
Ezekiel Pond
George Potwine
Sergt. Truman Powell
Sergt. Simeon Presbrey
Silas Reynolds
William Sergeant
Elijah Shaw
John Shirtliff
John Stearns
Jonathan Stickney
Jacob Truax
Jeremiah Utley
Peter Verano
Jeremiah Virginia
Isaiah Washburne
Edward Whitmore
Salmon Willoughby
Asa Willson
Perez Wright

GRAND ISLE COUNTY.

John Bush
John Knight
Joseph Phelps
James Sternberger
Stephen Sweet
Sergt. Church Tabor

ORANGE COUNTY.

Reuben Adams
Amaziah Ainsworth
Sluman Allen
Walcott Allyn
Aaron Andrews
Nathaniel Avery
Jesse Bailey
William Ballou
Sergt. George Barfield
Moses Bartholomew
Aaron Bayley
Peter Bayley
Josiah Bigelow
Barna Biglow

Ezra Blasdell
John Brown
William Brown
Sylvester Bugbee
John Bushnell
David Carlton
William Carlisle
Elias Carpenter
John Carpenter
Jonathan Carpenter
Cephas Child
Sergt. Joseph Clark
Forest Cloud
Lemuel Coburn
Jesse Cogswell
Enoch Colton
John Colton
Francis Davis
Sergt. Edward Dodge
Cushman Downer
James Downer
Amos Dwinell
Eliab Edson
Ariel Egerton
Samuel Eggleston
Benjamin Falch
Josiah Flagg
William Freeman
Zebulon Gitchell
John Guild
Daniel Hackett
Asa Hatch
Isaac Heath
John Hobart
Roger Hovey
Sergt. Samuel Hovey
Perley Howe
Aaron Hurd
Seth Hunt
Hiram Huntington
Abijah Hutchinson
Ichabod Hyde
Joseph Jenkins
Samuel Johnson
Phineas Kellogg
Israel Kibbie
Patrick Kennedy
Jonathan Ladd
Levi Leavitt
Lieut. John Lyman
Benjamin Martin

Joshua Martin
John Matson
Thomas McKnight
Nathaniel Morrill
Sergt. James Morris
Moses Morse
Elisha Newhall
William Nutt
Daniel Nye
Nathaniel Oak
Samuel Odway
Richard Paine
Capt. Samuel Paine
Edward Pease
Daniel Perkins
Elisha Philips
Sergt. Isaac Pinney
Samuel Plumley
James Pressey
Israel Putnam
Job Reed
Sergt. William Rolfe
Asa Smith
Roswell Smith
Ambrose Stebbins
Lieut. Mansfield Tappan
Sergt. Ashbel Tucker
Jonah Washburn
Amos Wheeler
Eli White
Elijah Whitney
William Wight

ORLEANS COUNTY.

Serg't James Adams
John Adams
Elijah Allen
Martin Allen
Jonathyn Allyn
Martin Barney
Christopher Bartlett
Joel Benton
Sergt. David Blanchard
Benjamin Burton
Bowman Chadwick
Isaac Child
John Clifford
Samuel Cobb
Phineas Cowles
Serg't William Craigue

John Currier
Lieut. Joseph Curtis
Daniel Davidson
Jonathan Foster
Silas French
Daniel Frost
Samuel Henry
Frederick W. Herman
Isaac Hinman
Joseph Hyde
John Keison
William Lang
George Little
James Little
John Mills
Nathan Nye
Serg't Aaron Parker
Andrew Peabody
Joseph Priest
Qm. Eber Robinson
Jonathan Robinson
Peter Sanborn
Joseph Scott
Amos Smith
Nehemiah Snow
Barzilla Spaulding
Lemuel Sturdevant
Stephen Tilden
Serg't Robert Trumbull
Benjamin Walker
Robert Waterman
Serg't Joseph E. Westgate
Nathan Willcox
Caleb Young

RUTLAND COUNTY.

Peter Ames
Moses Ambler
Asa Anderson
Oliver Arnold
Martin Ashley
Isaac Atwood
Daniel Ballard
Lemuel Barden
Philbrook Barrows
Silas Bartlett
Nicholas Barton
Samuel Bennett
Simeon Biglow
Caleb Blanchard
Serg't Timothy Boardman
Consider Bowen

Enos Briggs
Asa Brown
Daniel Buell
Lieut. Levi Buell
Joseph Burk
William Burnam
Samuel Burnell
Asa Carver
Rufus Carver
Wait Chatterton
Serg't Penuel Child
Caleb Churchill
Nathaniel Churchill
Ezra Clark
Ichabod G. Clark
John Collins
Serg't Abel Cooper
Royall Crowley
Serg't Joseph Daggett
Serg't David Dana
Asa Darbe
Enos Dean
Serg't Nathan Denison
William Dowe
James Dowling
Joshua Durant
Walter Durfee
Joel Earle
Serg't Eli Eastman
Abram Eaton
Daniel Eaton
Enoch Eaton
Serg't Jesse Eddy
Jotham Ford
Peter Fox
Nathan Freeman
Pearson Freeman
Serg't Amasa Fuller
Serg't Eli Gale
Serg't Nehemiah Gates
Serg't Samuel Gates
Solomon Gibbs
Simeon Gilbert
William Gilkey
John Godding
Daniel Goodenow
Serg't Simeon Goodrich
Thomas Gould
Serg't Andrew Grant
David Graves

William Graves
Serg't Allen Green
Peleg Green
Uzziah Green
Samuel Griswold
Hilkiah Grout
Peter Hall
John Hamblin
Thomas Hammond
Uriah Harrington
Richard Haskins
Joseph Hawkins
Moses Hawkins
Reuben Heath
Minor Hilyard
Jeremiah Hoit
Serg't Titus Holmes
Samuel Hooker
Serg't Abel Horton
John Howe
Caleb Howland
Zebulon Jewetts
Ozias Johnson
Oliver Ide
Lent Ives
Preserved Kellogg
Nathaniel Keyes
Peter Keyes
Serg't Elias King
Theodore King
Joel Knapp
Levi Larkin
Josiah Lawrence
Serg't Abel Lewis
Elijah Lillie
Stephen Long
Ezekiel Longley
Oliver Loomis
Eleazer Lyman
Willard Mann
Seth Martin
John McDonald
Jonathan Merrill
David Meriam
Samuel S. Merriman
John V. Miller
Serg't Caleb Morgon
Sergt. Solomon Moulton
Elias Munger
Serg't Benjamin Needham

Joseph Newell
Theodore Newell
James Noble
John Noble
William Noble
Jonathan Orms
Samuel Owen
Henry Packer
Serg't Abel Paine
Ephraim Parker
Serg't Samuel Parker
Thomas Parmenter
Eliphalet Patee
Isaac Peck
John Pepper
Israel Phillips
Serg't Daniel Platt
Elias Post
Serg't Simeon Post
Serg't Caleb Potter
Daniel Potter
Serg't John Potter
Zimri Pratt
Lieut. Silas Procter
William Putrin
John Randall
Jonathan Remington
Lieut. Jonathan Reynolds
Lieut. Jonas Rice
Jonas Rich
Stephen Richardson
Bela Rogers
Lieut. Charles Rogers
Jeremiah Rogers
Thomas Rogers
Serg't Moses Root
Serg't Rufus Ross
John Scott
Elijah Seger
David Shipherd
Jesse Slayton
Isaac Southworth
Jasher Southworth
Aaron Smith
Pliny Smith
Isaac Spalding
Ebenezer Squires
Asa Staples
Simeon Stevens
Gould Stiles
Abel Taft

Serg't Gideon Terney
Thomas Todd
Serg't John Tolman
Elijah Trull
Wait Tucker
James Walker
Stephen Ward
Thomas Ward
Eleazer Warner
Phinehas Whitney
Joel Willis
Serg't Silas Willis
David Wood
Henry Woodhouse
Amos Yeaw
Simeon Young

WASHINGTON COUNTY.

Moses Ainsworth
Asahel Allen
Abiather Austin
Zebedee Beckley
James Britain
Eliada Brown
John Brown
Ezra Butler
Joseph Buzzell
Thomas Cutler
Ebenezer Dodge
Abel Dustin
Serg't Thomas Foster
Thomas French
Benjamin Fuller
Serg't Josiah Goodell
Gilbert Hatch
Reuben Hawks
Samuel Henderson
Stephen Jones
Enos Kellogg
Martin Kellogg
Serg't Elias Kingsley
Elisha Lathrop
Jeremiah Leland
Jesse Martin
John Mellen
Aaron Miner
Joshua Morrill
John Morse
Daniel Moses
Andrew Nealey

Robert Parker
Azel Parkhurst
Peter Reed
Phinehas Rider
Timothy Roberts
Amos Robinson
Serg't Asher Robinson
Noah Robinson
Abial Shattuck
Joseph Sherman
Abraham Shipman
Amasa Skinner
Eli Skinner
Jared Skinner
Darius Spaulding
Silas Spalding
Ephraim Stone
Edmund Town
Elisha Town
James Town
James Twing
Samuel Upham
Curwin Wallis
Philip White
Elisha Wilcox
Ephraim Willey
Serg't Uriah Wilkins
Elijah Wright
Jonathan Wright

WINDHAM COUNTY.

Hezekiah Abbey
Samuel Adams
William Bartlett
John Bemis
Samuel Bennett
Serg't William Black
Serg't Lamech Blauden
David Blood
David Bond
Phinehas Bond
Darius Bullock
Israel Bullock
John Carpenter
James Case
Serg't Samuel Chaffin
Henry Chandler
Hiel Chandler
Nathaniel Cheney
Charles Colton

Simeon Conant
Elisha Cook
Joseph Crumb
Joshua Davis
Samuel Davis
Archelaus Dean
Joseph Dunton
Maverick Eaton
Elijah Elmer
Colton Evans
Pearley Fairbanks
Eliphalet Felt
Abiah Fuller
Benjamin Furniss
Asa Gale
Nahum Goodenow
Abel Grant
Serg't Amos Gray
Ellis Griffith
Jesse Guild
Ephraim Hall
John Harris
Levi Hayward
Jonas Hazeltine
Samuel Hiscock
Abraham Hill
Joel Hill
Ephraim Holden
Elihu Hotchkiss
Jonathan Huntley
Edmund Ingalls
William Jenison
Amos Joy
Serg't Eleazer Kendall
John Kidder
Nathan Knowlton
Henry Lake
Moses Larnard
Samuel Larrebee
Abner Lewis
Reuben Lippinwell
Jesse Marsh
William Marsh
Phinehas Mather
Rufus Moore
Elijah Morse
Benjamin Murdock
Joseph Muzzy
Marshall Newton
Jabez Paine
Ebenezer Parker

Samuel Parker
Andrew Parsons
Levi Perry
Francis Phelps
John Philips
Oliver Philips
Elijah Pike
George Porter
Amos Prouty
William Ranney
Ezekiel Ransom
Benjamin Reed
Serg't Frederick Reed
Mark Richards
William Robinson
Samuel Rockwood
Lieut. Joseph Rodgers
Zepheniah Shepardson
Serg't Asa Smith
David Smith
Ebenezer Smith
Ephraim Smith
Hezekiah Smith
John Smith
Samuel Spaulding
John Stearns
Serg't William Stearns
John Stowell
Joel Streeter
Ebenezer Taft
William Taft
Amasa Tiffany
David Tottingham
Joseph Tuttle
Sergt. Samuel Viall
James Walker
Serg't Beriah Wheeler
Abiel Whitman
John Wier
Aaron Wilder
Samuel Wiswall
Artemas Woodard
Jonathan Woolley

WINDSOR COUNTY.

Joseph Abbott
Timothy Adams
John Adye
Israel Aikin
John Aikin

Noah Aldrich
Quartus Alexander
Phineas Alvord
Matthew Atherton
John Austin
John Austin
    (not a duplicate)
Samuel Axtel
Lyman Bache
Stephen Backus
Stephen Baker
Isaac Baldwin
Jason Banister
Dan Barnard
Joel Barret
Serg't Luther Bartholomew
Thomas Bayley
Josiah Belknap
Amos Bemis
John Bennett
Samuel Bennett
William Bennett
John Billings
Isaac Bisbee
Levi Bishop
Jonathan M. Bissell
Serg't Josiah Blake
John Blood
Lieut. Benjamin Bosworth
Jewett Boyington
William Bragg
Chaplain Daniel Breck
Reuben Brooks
Solomon Brown
Joel Burbank
Silas Burdoo
Nathaniel Burgess
Ebenezer Burnham
William Butman
Manessah Cady
Nedabiah Cady
Abel Camp
Barnabas Caswell
Josiah Chandler
William Chandler
Serg't Calvin Chapin
Gideon Chapin
John Chase
Moses Chase
Serg't Waldo Cheney
Lyman Child

Joshua Church
Benjamin Clark
Serg't Daniel Clark
Squier Cleveland
Samuel Cleveland
Stephen Cleveland
Nathan Cobb
David Colburn
Solomon Coleman
Oliver Cook
Edward Corlew
Bibye L. Cotton
Serg't Thomas Craig
Serg't Thomas Craige
Amos Crain
Noah Crocker
Holmes Cushman
Daniel Davis
Joel Davis
James L. Dean
Jeremiah Dean
Darius Dewey
Martin Diggins
Samuel Dike
Asahel Doubleday
Gershom Dunham
David Edgerton
Serg't Enoch Emerson
Solomon Emmons
Nathaniel Farr
Elijah Farrington
Thomas Fay
Nathan Felch
Stephen Fisk
Daniel Fletcher
Abel Fling
Jacob Foster
Joseph Foster
Rufus Foster
Edmund Freeman
Joseph French
Josiah Gibbs
Stephen Gibbs
Sergt. William Gibson
John Giddings
Peter Gilson
Asa Green
Isaac Green
Luther Grover
Zebedee Hackett

Henry Hall
Serg't Jacob Hall
Jonathan Hall
John Haraden
William Harlow
Samuel Harrington
Luke Harris
Jacob Haskill
John Haskel
Prince Haskell
Serg't Adrian Hatch
Josiah Hatch
Joseph Hawkins
Solomon Hayward
Solomon Hazen
Ephraim Heald
Isaac Hincher
Seth Hodges
Lieut. Thomas Hodgkins
Ebenezer Hoisington
Samuel Howe
Joseph Hulett
Jonathan Ingersoll
Calvin Johnson
Jonathan Jones
Josiah Jordan
Simeon Keith
Isaac Kendall
Jacob Kendall
Serg't Elias Keyes
John Kibling
Serg't Daniel King
Oliver Lauthrop
Surgeon Joseph Lewis
Darius Liscomb
Caleb Litchfield
Daniel Lovejoy
Simeon Loverin
Ezra Lowell
Asa Lull
David Lumbard
John Lumbard
Alvan Marcy
Chester Marcey
Gardener Marcey
Henry McNelly
Samuel Metcalf
Anderson Miner
David Morehouse
Serg't Aaron Mosher

Israel Newton
David Nichols
William Nichols
Dan Niles
Elisha Orcutt
Oliver Osgood
James Parker
Stephen Parsival
Justin Parsons
Joseph Patterson
Moses Peabody
John Perkins
Walter Pollard
Simeon Pomeroy
Serg't Asahel Powers
Thomas Powers
Asa Pratt
Nathan Pratt
Thomas Prentiss
Timothy Proctor
Ezra Putnam
Stephen Reed
Joseph Remington
Eliakim Rice
Jason Rice
Samuel Robbins
Henry Robey
Serg't Reuben Robinson
Eliphalet Rogers
Juduthun Rogers
John Root
Elijah Royce
Jeremiah Rust
Oliver Rust
George Sampson
Philemon Sampson
Silas Sears
Calvin Seaver
Ebenezer Severance
Lemuel Shaw
Daniel Sherwin
Samuel Shipman
Joshua Simmons
Luther Skinner

Asahel Smith
Paul Smith
Abraham Snow
Thomas Southgate
Ezra Spaulding
Gardner Spooner
Philip Sprague
Seth Sterling
David Stimson
Nathaniel Stone
Timothy Stone
William Strong
Joseph Taggart
Joseph Taylor
Leonard Taylor
Josiah Tilden
Isaiah Tinkham
Seth Tinkham
Benjamin Thatcher
Andrew Thomas
Peleg Thomas
John Thurston
Lyman Tolman
James Topliff
James Tracy
Nahum Trask
Serg't Retire Trask
Serg't John Wallace
Abraham Waterman
Elisha Waterman
Serg't William Waterman
Daniel Weatherbee
Jesse Williams
Thomas Williams
Sylvanus Willis
Solomon Wilson
Jonathan Whitcomb
Andrew White
Solomon White
Joseph Wood
Peter Woodbury
Asa Wright
Nathaniel Wright

NAMES OF REVOLUTIONARY SOLDIERS BURIED IN VERMONT.

Compiled by Walter H. Crockett, of St. Albans, Secretary of the Vermont Society, Sons of the American Revolution, additional to the list printed in the Proceedings of the Vermont Historical Society for 1903-04.

Addison.

Lorain Evarts,
Samuel Pond,
Jacob Post,
John Strong.

Albany.

Marshall Pillsbury,
Samuel Russell,
Ebenezer Watson.

Alburgh.

Ichabod Babcock,
John Babcock.

Andover.

Joseph Abbott,
Jonas Adams,
Luther Adams,
Peter Adams,
Hart Balch,
John Barton,
David Burton,
Jonathan Crane,
Joseph Dodge,
Ebenezer Farnsworth,
David Hazleton,
Solomon Howard,
Daniel Knight,
Samuel Manning,

Jesse Parkhurst,
Peter Putnam,
Joseph Stickney,
Samson Walker,
Moses Warner.

Arlington.

Constant Barney,
Ephraim Blowers,
Israel Burritt,
John Calkins,
Capt. Martin Deming,
John Gray,
Benoni Hawkins,
Simeon Littlefield.

Athens.

Ezra Chaffee,
Charles Colton,
George Porter.

Bakersfield.

Aaron Barlow,
Joshua Barnes,
Jonathan Farnsworth,
Foster Paige,
Maj. Elisha Parker.

Baltimore.

Seth Houghton.

Barnard.

Samuel Bennett,
William Bennett,
Hollan Blackmer,
Jacob Boyden,
William Buckman,
William Chamberlin,
Moses Davis,
Robert Dean,
John Foster,
Peter Foster,
Elisha Freeman,
William Freeman,
Sergt. Charles French,
William Harlow,
Ezra Spaulding,
Samuel Stewart.

Barnet.

Levi Hall,
Stephen Rider,
John Waddell.

Benson.

Bristol Bennett,
Rufus Ewen,
Eli King,
Timothy Prince.

Berkshire.

Arthur Danow,
Levi Darling,
John Perley,

Ezekiel Pond,
Elisha Shaw,
Edward Whitmore.

Berlin.

Allen Andrews,
Elijah Andrews,
Daniel Hayden,
Job Reed,
Lemuel Stickney.

Bethel.

Jason Bannister,
Moses Bragg,
Reuben Brooks,
Stephen Cleveland,
Bibye Cotton,
Amos Crain,
Stephen Fisk,
Joel Marsh,
Nehemiah Noble,
Ezra Putnam,
Benajah Strong.

Bloomfield.

Adin Bartlett.

Braintree.

Edward Bass,
Simeon Curtis,
Elijah Huntington,
Thomas Kenney,
Matthew Pratt.

Barre.

Daniel Averill,
William Farwell,
Elisha Gale,
Ebenezer Putnam,
Col. Enos Walker.

Barton.

John Adams,
Benoni Burnham,
Joseph Hyde,
John Monsam,
Jonathan Robinson,
Lemuel Sturtevant.

Belvidere.

Moses Brown,
Eliphalet Carpenter,
John Rosier.

Bennington.

David Avery,
Caleb Austin,
Ephraim Bowen,
Cornelius Bracy,
Solomon Clark,
Charles Cushman,
Aaron Deming,
Jeremiah Field,
Job Greene,
Peter Hardwood,
Simeon Harvey,
David Hinman,
Benjamin Hoadley,
Jesse Loomis,
Abner Noble,
Lieut. John Noble,
Martin Norton,
Jonathan Robinson,
Samuel Rockwood,
Samuel Safford,
Simeon Thayer,
Isaac Tichenor,
Col. Ebenezer Walbridge.

Bradford.

John Putnam,
Arad Stebbins.

Brandon.

Simeon Bigelow,
William Dodge,
Stephen Durkee,
Zeeb Green,
Nathaniel Harris,
Solomon Hinds,
Jonathan Merriam,
Ebenezer Squires,
Roger Smith.

Brattleboro.

Elnathan Allen,
John Carpenter,
Stephen Greenleaf,

Ruthford Hayes,
Reuben King,
George Loveland,
Ephraim Nash,
Asa Putnam,
Daniel Stearns,
Reuben Stearns.

Bridgewater.

Isaac Bisbee,
George Boyce,
Joseph Boyce,
James Crooker,
George Denison,
Sergt. Sam'l Denison,
Daniel Dike,
James Fletcher,
Seth Fletcher,
Joseph French,
Josiah Gibbs,
Elisha Gilbert,
Asa Green,
Capt. John Hawkins,
Asa Jones,
Stephen Knowlton,
Rowland Leonard,
Amos Murdell,
Thomas Palmer,
Benjamin Perkins,
Nathan Pratt,
Eleazer Robinson,
Phineas Sanderson,
Beriah Smith,
Thomas Southgate,
Noah Thompson,
James Topliff.

Bridport.

David Cory,
Asa Hemenway,
Jacob Hemenway,
Samuel Hemenway,
Phineas Kitchell,
Sergt. Abel Rice,
Dr. William Vaughn.

Bristol.

Rufus Barnard,
Joseph Bird,
Walcott Burnham,

Jeriah Chamberlin,
John Corry,
Ebenezer Cushman,
Robert Dunshee,
Cyprian Eastman,
Asahel Hall,
Samuel Hall,
Jeremiah Hatch,
John D. Holly,
Paul P. Holly,
William Howden,
Jeremiah Mead,
Asaph Parmelee,
Benjamin Plumley,
Amos Scott,
Abraham Vreedenburgh,
David Whitney.

Brookline.

Samuel Bennett,
Eleazer Cushman,
Luther Newcomb.

Brookfield.

Reuben Adams,
Barna Bigelow,
Experians Fisk, Jr.,
Nathan Fisk,
Timothy Kendall,
John Paine,
Noah Paine.

Brownington.

Humphrey Nichols,
Joel Priest,
Isaac Smith,
Samuel Smith.

Brunswick.

Simeon Wait.

Burke.

Seth Clark,
Abner Coe,
Sergt. Benj. Farner,
Daniel Hall,
Sergt. Isaac Martin.

Burlington.

Alanson Adams,
John Adams,
Reuben Bostwick,
Capt. Amos Burnham,
Daniel Castle,
Samuel Hitchcock,
William Kilbourne,
John Pierce,
Nathan Seymour.

Cabot.

Moses Ainsworth,
Benjamin Andrews,
Eliphalet Bill,
Joseph Hoyt.

Calais.

Solomon Janes.

Cambridge.

James Campbell,
Amos Fassett,
John Fassett, Jr.,
Elihu Grant,
Benjamin Griswold,
Parker Page,
Joel F. Perham,
Sergt. Truman Powell.

Canaan.

Gilman Clough,
Oliver Goss,
John Hughs,
John Weeks.

Castleton.

Joseph Babcock,
William Bromley,
William Cushman,
Sgt. Jonathan Deming,
Daniel Eaton,
Preserved Kellogg,
Daniel Lowden.

Cavendish.

Benjamin Adams,
Timothy Adams,

Isaac Baldwin,
Samuel Burbank,
Capt. John Coffeen,
Joel Davis,
Nathaniel Fair,
Asaph Fletcher,
Nehemiah Green,
John McLane,
Elnathan Reed,
William Spalding,
Samuel Stearns,
Oliver Whitney.

Charleston.

John Palmer,
William Sawyer.

Charlotte.

Isaac Cogswell,
Ephraim Page,
Stephen Turrill.

Chelsea.

Sherman Allen,
Ananiah Bohonon,
Abraham Brigham,
Daniel Buck,
Benjamin Burgess,
Frederick Calkins,
Asa Dearborn,
Hiram Huntington,
William Killown,
John Martin,
Thomas Parker,
David Perry.

Chester.

Benjamin Blaney,
Nathan Boyden,
Thomas Caryl,
Joshua Church,
Ephraim Clark,
Jeremiah Dean,
Stephen Dyer,
David Earl,
Timothy Eastman,
Ebenezer Farrington,
Daniel Fletcher,
Paul Fletcher,

Surg. Laban Gates,
Moses Gile,
Joshua Jordan,
Simeon Keith,
John Kibling,
Archelous Putnam,
John Putnam,
Stephen Randall,
Waitstill Ranney,
Reuben Ray,
Jason Rice,
Stephen Riggs,
Ezra Sargent,
Jabez Sargent,
William Stoodley,
John Thurston,
Amasa Turner,
Richard Ward,
Amos Weatherby,
Benjamin Whitmore,
Solomon Wilson.

Chittenden.

Asa Durkee.

Clarendon.

Sergt. Abel Horton,
Dr. David Palmer,
Ephraim Parker,
Sergt. Samuel Parker,
Isaac Southworth,
Jesse Sprague,
Lewis Walker.

Colchester.

Alexander Alford,
Jeremiah Fisher,
Peter Gale,
John Law,
Amos Mansfield, Jr.,
Claud Monty,
Amos Preston,
Lemuel Tubbs,
David Webster.

Concord.

Joseph Ball,
Elias Cheney,
Jonathan Corser,

Josiah Goodale,
David Hibbard,
Hinds Reed,
Noah Vilas,
Capt. Samuel Wetherbe,
Capt. Samuel Witherell.

Corinth.

Jeremiah Dewey,
Eleazer Porter,
Eleazer P. Putnam.

Cornwall.

Jared Abernethy,
John Alvord,
John Boynton,
Joseph Cogswell,
Isaiah Gilbert,
Reuben Hall,
Israel C. Jones,
Gideon Miller,
Reuben Peck,
William Pratt,
John Rockwell,
William Samson,
Daniel Scovel,
William Ward.

Coventry.

Frederick W. Herman,
David Lathe,
Joseph Priest,
Edward Welch.

Craftsbury.

Capt. Ebenezer Crafts,
Daniel Davison,
John Hadley,
Joseph Scott,
Sergt. Rob't Trumbull.

Danby.

Bradford Barnes,
Minor Hilyard,
Elijah Lilly,

Danville.

Uri Babbit,
Jethro Batchelder,
Jesse Cheney,
Thomas Colby,
Jonathan Danforth,
Salma Davis,
Benjamin Deming,
Stephen Dexter,
Samuel Hawley,
Thomas Hoyt,
John Rollins,
Ebenezer Sawyer,
Caleb Stiles,
Joseph Tilton.

Derby.

Abram Alexander,
Simon Davis,
John Healey,
Isaac Hinman,
Timothy Hinman,
Simeon Pope.

Dorset.

Peletiah Dewey,
Benedict Eggleston,
Asa Farwell,
Isaac Farwell,
Asahel L. Fenton,
Noah Fuller,
John Sargent,
Benjamin Tenney,
James Wrin.

Dover.

Benjamin Baldwin,
Balah Kendall,
Capt. Elijah Stearns.

Dummerston.

Daniel Bemis,
John Bemis,
Nathaniel Bixby,
Thomas Boyden,
William Boyden,
Ellis Griffith,
John Reed,

William Robertson,
Daniel Tenney.

Duxbury.

John Colt.

East Montpelier.

Eseck Howland.

Eden.

Jonas Harrington,
Eli Hinds, Jr.,
Isaac Lackey,
Samuel Plumley,
Peter Wylie.

Elmore.

Ebenezer Copin.

Enosburg.

Job Libbey,
James Miller.

Essex.

France Faxon.

Fairfax.

James Bellows,
Archibald Cook,
Joseph Cross,
E. Faxon,
George Majors,
Israel Richardson,
Bradstreet Spafford.

Fairfield.

Whitmore Beardsley,
Jabez Burr,
Oliver Cleveland,
Abel Fairbanks,
Jabez Hawkins,
Josiah Osgood,
Philip Priest,
Silas Safford,
Dyer Sherwood.

Fair Haven.

Samuel Stannard.

Fayston.

William Newcomb.

Ferrisburg.

Daniel Champion,
Josiah Johnson,
William Kellogg,
Abel Thompson,
Nathan Walker.

Fletcher.

Daniel Bailey,
Henry Campbell,
Samuel Danforth,
Rufus Montague.

Franklin.

Paul Gates.

Georgia.

Capt. Jonat'n Danforth,
Loammi Pattee,
John Wood,
Reuben Wood.

Glover.

Paul Cook,
Paul Hardy.
Jesse Thomas,

Goshen.

Enoch Reynolds.

Grand Isle.

Capt. John Stark.

Granville.

Abiathar Austin,
Eli Lewis,
Abraham Parker,
James Shaw,
Jeremiah Snow,

Grafton.

David Blood,
Simeon Conant,
Nathaniel Cutler,
Henry Davis,
David French,
Abraham Gibson,
David Gibson,
Jonathan Gibson,
Solomon Gibson,
Enoch Hale,
John Kidder,
Samuel Spaulding,
William Stickney,
Joseph Thatcher,
Jonathan Warner,
Samuel Whitney,
Asa M. Wyman.

Greensboro.

Samuel Badger,
John Cross,
Amos Smith,
Lieut. Thos. Tolman.

Groton.

John Clark,
Ebenezer Fisk.

Guildhall.

John Cook,
Capt. Benoni Cutler,
David Denison,
Moses Hale,
David Hopkinson,
Samuel Howe.

Guilford.

Nehemiah Andrews,
Daniel Boyden,
James Boyden,
Ebenezer Chamberlain,
Jeremiah Graves,
Thomas Harris,
Samuel Larabee,
William Marsh,
Cyrus Martin,
Jasper Patridge,

Adonijah Putnam,
Micah Rice,
Seth Rice,
Eliel Washburn,
Aaron Wilder.

Halifax.

Thomas Adams,
James Babcock,
Abner Bemis,
Joel Cutler,
John Farnham,
David Goodall,
Jesse Guild,
John Harris,
Israel Jones,
Moses Larned,
Francis Phelps,
Elijah Pike,
Newton Ransom,
Hezekiah Smith,
Eleazer Whitney,
Artemas Woodard.

Hancock.

Charles Church,
Capt. Nath'l Cushman.

Hardwick.

Charles Bailey,
Abel Carpenter,
Abel Conant,
Jonathan Curtis,
John Fox,
Sergt. Thomas Fuller,
Sergt. David Norris,
Eleazer Nutting,
Samuel Stevens,
Joseph Weeks,
Reuben Wheatley.

Hartford.

Sgt. Luth. Bartholomew,
Daniel Beard,
Capt. William Bramble,
James Call,
Simeon Chapman,
David Coburn (or Col-
    burn),

Joshua Dewey,
Shadrack Dodge,
Lieut. Israel Gillet,
John Gillet,
Sergt. Jacob Hall,
Willis Hall,
Samuel Harrington,
Daniel Hazen,
Elijah Hazen,
Hezekiah Hazen,
Capt. Joshua Hazen,
Solomon Hazen,
Thomas Hazen,
Benjamin Hoyt,
Capt. Abel Marsh,
Daniel Marsh,
Eliphalet Marsh,
Elisha Marsh,
John Marsh,
Col. Joseph Marsh,
David Newton,
John Paddock,
Samuel Pease,
Daniel Pineo,
Eliot Porter,
Rowland Powell,
Amos Richardson,
Thomas Richardson,
Amos Robinson,
Francis W. Savage,
Seth Savage,
Thomas Savage,
Darius Sessions,
Philip .Sprague,
Solomon Strong,
William Strong,
Sergt. Andrew Tacy,
Reuben Tenney,
Josiah Tilden,
Oliver Udall.

Hartland.

Noah Aldrich,
Eldad Alexander,
Quartus Alexander,
Simeon Alford,
Wm. Symmes Ashley,
Thomas Bagley,
Moses Barron,
John Billings,
Nathan Billings,

Eliazer Bishop,
Chap. Daniel Breck,
Solomon Brown,
Isaiah Burk,
Jonathan Burk,
Marston Cabot,
Nathan Call,
Samuel Capron,
Lieut. Ephraim Carey,
Capt. Nathaniel Cole,
Melvin Cotton,
Thomas Cotton,
Holmes Cushman,
Ichabod Cushman,
Col. George Denison,
John Dunsmore,
Asahel Doubleday,
John Dunbar,
Robert Dunbar,
Elisha Flower,
William Flower,
Elisha Gallup,
William Gallup,
Zelates Gates,
Peter Gibson,
Peter Gilson,
Joseph Grow,
Samuel Hearley,
Thomas Hoadley,
Jonathan Hodgman,
Maj. Lot Hodgman,
Phineas Killam,
Thomas Lawton,
Darius Liscomb,
Nehemiah Liscomb,
John Lull,
Timothy Lull,
Isaac Maine,
Gardner Marcy,
Joseph Marcy,
Isaac Morgan,
Robert Morrison,
John Robbins,
Eliphalet Rogers,
Isaac Sargent,
Lemuel Scott,
Thomas Shaw,
Jesse Smeed,
Leonard Spaulding,
Lieut. Daniel Spooner,
Eliakim Spooner,

Paul Spooner,
John Sumner,
Asa Taylor,
Nathaniel Waldron,
Jonathan Whitney,
Capt. Aaron Willard,
Oliver Willard,
Abel Wright,
Zadock Wright.

Highgate.

Philip Shelters.

Hinesburgh.

Moses Dow,
Asa Forbes,
John Green,
Dan Howard,
Jonathan Stearns,
Eliphaz Steel.

Holland.

John Bishop,
Isaac Clement,
Qm. Eber Robinson,
Isaac Sargent.

Huntington.

Ebenezer Cutler,
Zebediah Joslin,
John Moses,
Jonas Shattuck.

Hyde Park.

John Collins,
John McCloud.

Ira.

Joseph Tower,

Irasburgh.

Benjamin Barton,
Amos Conant,
Benjamin Hardy.

Jamaica.

John Bradley,
Nathaniel Cheney,

Timothy Fisher,
Ichabod Higgins,
Joel Hill,
Bailey Rawson,
Gideon Stoddard.

Jericho.

Peter L. Allen,
Isaac Benham,
Ichabod Burnham,
Benoni Chapin,
Ichabod Chapin,
Noah Chittenden,
Simeon Davis,
Azariah Rood,
Roger Stevens,
J. I. Warner.

Johnson.

William Boyes,
Solomon Briggs,
Jonathan Burnham,
——— Chase,
Elisha Dodge,
Ralph Ellingwood,
David Erwin,
William Heath,
Jonathan McConnell,
Jeremiah McDaniel,
Samuel Miller,
Daniel Perkins,
Arunah Waterman.

Kirby.

Zebulon Burroughs,
Jonathan Lewis,
Asa Parker,
Stephen Watkins.

Landgrove.

David Carpenter,
Hezekiah Ward Clark,
Ephraim Hildreth,
Reuben Holt.

Leicester.

Isaac Atwood,
Benjamin Whitman.

Lincoln.

Joshua Rugg.

Londonderry.

Abraham Abbott,
David Cochran,
Bithiah Howard,
Edmund Ingalls,
Lincoln Stiles,
Jeremiah Wheeler,
Nathan Whiting.

Lowell.

Jonathan Powers.

Ludlow.

Sergt. Levi Adams,
Ephraim Dutton,
Jesse Fletcher,
Josiah Fletcher,
Josiah F. Richardson,
John Spafford,
Jesse Spaulding,
Thomas Weatherby,
Jonathan Whitcomb.

Lunenburgh.

Louis Cook,
Zuriah Marshall,
Samuel Martin,
Samuel Nash,
Timothy Nash,
Azariah Webb.

Lyndon.

John Bly,
Ozias Caswell,
Stephen Eastman,
Moses Evans,
Erastus Harvey,
Oliver Hartwell,
Sergt. Henry Hoffman,
Jacob Houghton,
Ebenezer Howland,
Jona. Locklin,
John McGaffey,
William Miles,

Rufus Moore,
Ephraim Niles,
Job Olney,
Sergt. Gaias Peck,
Nathaniel Phillips,
Elijah Ross,
Moses Root,
James Sherman,
Jonas Sprague,
Jonathan Swan.

Maidstone.

Sergt. Jacob Schoff.

Manchester.

Samuel Mitchell,
Gideon Moody,
Sergt. Eli Pettibone,
Samuel Walker.

Marlboro.

James Cutler,
Boomer Jenks,
Erastus Mather,
Phineas Mather,
John Philips,
Amos Prouty,
Jonas Whitney.

Marshfield.

Joshua Cheney,
Ebenezer Dodge,
Joseph T. Eaton,
Stephen Rich.

Mendon.

Hilkiah Grout,
Isaac Sanderson.

Middlebury.

Sergt. Ethan Andrews,
Jonathan Blin,
Alpheus Brooks,
Justus Cobb,
Samuel Cook,
James Crane,
George Griswold,

Calvin Goodno,
Robert Huxton,
Bela Manzer,
Ely Nichols,
Elijah Olmstead,
Benoni Shurtleff,
Jesse Spencer,
Seth Storrs,
Israel Wadsworth.

Middlesex.

Jeremiah Clark,
Jeremiah Leland,
Ebenezer Putnam.

Middletown Springs.

Jedediah Edgerton,
Richard Hoskins,
David Parker,
Gamaliel Waldo.

Milton.

Benjamin Adams,
John Blake,
Thomas Dewey,
Elihu Herrick,
William Hewes,
Oliver Howard,
Elisha Owen.

Monkton.

William Niles,
Lieut. Daniel Spooner,
William Spooner,
John Stearns,
Lemuel Tracy.

Montgomery.

Lieut. John Clapp,
Bliss Hoisington,
John A. Ripley,
Joshua Wade.

Montpelier.

Elias Metcalf,
John Putnam,
Edward West.

Morgan.

Joshua Bailey,
Nathaniel S. Clark,
James Taylor,
Nathan Wilcox.

Moretown.

John Burdick,
Joshua Freeman,
Joseph Haseltine,
Amos Spalding.

Morristown.

Elisha Bugbee,
John Cole,
Michajah Dunham,
James Little,
Joshua Merrill,
Comfort Olds,
William Small,
Adam Sumner,
Sergt. Jos. E. Westgate,
Thomas Youngman.

Mount Holly.

Joel Earle.

Mount Tabor.

Sergt. Joseph Daggett,
Gideon Tabor.

Newbury.

Peter Bagley,
Thomas Eastman,
David Haseltine,
Daniel Heath,
Joseph Herriman,
Samuel Johnson,
John Mellen,
Tarrant Putnam,
John Smith,
Asa Tenney,
David Tenney,
William Tice,
Charles P. Walker.

Newfane.

Jacob Allen,
Ephraim Hall,
William Hills,
William King,
Nathan Knowlton,
Zebediah Marsh,
Marshall Newton.

New Haven.

John Conant,
John Coon,
Elisha Fuller,
Ephraim Munson,
Joseph Prime,
Caleb Rich,
Simon Stickney,
Benjamin Taintor.

Newport.

Stephen Barnard,
John Jenness,
Archippus Wheeler.

Northfield.

Roswell Adams,
William Ashcroft,
Thomas Averill,
John Brown,
Aquila Jones,
Samuel Richardson,
Stanton Richardson,
Eliphus Shipman.

North Hero.

Samuel Doty,
Abram Woodard.

Norwich.

Daniel Baldwin,
Nath'l Boardman, Jr.,
Capt. Elijah Burton,
Henry Burton,
Jacob Burton,
Solomon Cushman,
Hezekiah Goodrich,
John Goodrich,
John Gould,

Joseph Howes,
Jerome Hutchinson,
Samuel Hutchinson,
Calvin Johnson,
Surg. Joseph Lewis,
David Lyman,
Timothy Nichols,
Daniel Nye,
Samuel Patridge,
Ebenezer Percival,
Jeremiah Percival,
Calvin Seaver,
Jonathan Spear,
Joel Stinson,
Mendwell Strong,
Joseph Tucker,
Solomon White.

Orange.

Nathaniel Bacheller,
Sgt. Jonathan Conant,
Samuel Judkins,
Samuel Richardson.

Orwell.

Jonathan Belden,
Thomas Eggleston,
Ira Kilbourn,
Billy Monger,
Capt. James Noble,
Sampson Spaulding.

Pawlet.

David Comstock,
Eldad Curtis,
Phineas Meigs,
Moses Porter,
Jacob Sacks,
Nathan Spalding.

Panton.

Rupee Bacheller,
Dan Smith,
William Shepherd.

Peacham.

Abijah Bailey,
James Bailey,
Hastings Blanchard,

Henry Blake,
Wells Burbank,
Abiel Chamberlain,
Col. John Chandler,
Edward Clark,
Samuel Davis,
Jonathan Elkins,
Judson Farrar,
Capt. Nathan Hurd,
Joab Kimball,
Ashbel Martin,
David Martin,
James Miner,
Lemuel Northrop,
John Skeele,
Ebenezer Spencer,
Simeon Walker.

Peru.

Benjamin Barnard,
Luther Barnard,
Aaron Dewey,
Peter Gould.

Pittsfield.

Josiah Babcock,
Sergt. Pennel Child,
Joseph Durkee,
Elijah Segar.

Pittsford.

Robert Andrews,
Davi Hall,
Thomas Hammond,
Amos Harwood,
Amos Lawrence,
Ezekiel Longley,
Dennis Miller,
Zebulon Pond,
Peter Powers,
Jeremiah Rann,
James Walker,
Rufus Wheeden,
Phineas Whitney,
Joel Willis,
Oliver Wolcott.

Plainfield.

Isaac Vincent.

Plymouth.

Samuel G. Allen,
Robert Bishop,
Sergt. Daniel Clark,
John Coolidge,
Henry Fletcher,
Benjamin Green,
John Mudge,
Caleb Snow.

Pomfret.

Elnathan Allen,
James Burnham,
Josiah Chandler,
John Cheadle,
William Child,
John W. Dana,
Eliphalet Fales,
Oliver Goff,
Timothy Harding,
Elijah Hoar,
Seth Hodges,
Elijah Mason,
Reuben D. Massey,
Matthew Miller,
Thomas Noonan,
Lieut. Ephraim Peake,
Abidah Smith,
John O. Thacher,
Isaiah Tinkham,
William Whitman,
Ebenezer Winslow.

Pownal.

John Downer,
Louis Dunham,
Obadiah Dunham,
Benjamin Grover,
Moses Hastings,
Zaccheus Hovey,
David Jepson,
John Magoon,
Benjamin Morgan,
Capt. Eli Noble,
John Noble,
Josiah Noble,
William Ray,
John Sherman,
Joseph Thorp.

Poultney.

Samuel Adams,
Azariah Dewey,
John Herrick,
Henry Hyde,
Abraham Kilbourne,
James Powers,
William Ward.

Putney.

Lieut. John Gates,
Benjamin Read,
Timothy Underwood,
Joseph Winslow.

Randolph.

Simeon Belknap,
Moses Bragg,
David Carpenter,
Jonathan Carpenter,
Jesse Cogswell,
John Cogswell,
Alvin Edson,
Sergt. Josiah Edson,
Isaac Grow,
John Hobart,
Joseph Morton,
Capt. Samuel Paine,
Moses Pearsons,
Samuel Steele,
Chancy L. Temple,
Nathaniel Throop,
Abner Weston,
Horace Wheeler,
Jonathan Wills.

Reading.

David Burnham,
Timothy Fullam,
Jonathan Jones,
William Morison,
Stephen Rice,
Thomas Townsend.

Readsboro.

Archilous Dean,
Ezra Keyes,
Ebenezer Stearns.

Richford.

Daniel Jones,
Gideon Wood.

Richmond.

Oliver Cutler,
Sergt. John Devereaux,
William Humphrey,
Daniel Robbins,
Bigford Spooner.

Rochester.

Thomas Bailey,
Josiah Chandler,
Timothy Clark,
David Clough,
Sergt. Enoch Emerson,
John McAllister,
Seth Tinkham,
Sergt. Retire Trask,
John Young.

Rockingham.

Philip Adams,
Benjamin Burt,
Charles Church,
Ebenezer Clark,
Nathaniel Clark,
Timothy Clark,
John Dudley,
John Fish,
Benjamin Gould,
Jacob Gould,
Ebenezer McAlvin,
Jonathan Morison,
Joseph Muzzy,
John Stearns,
Jonathan Stearns,
Sergt. William Stearns,
William Stearns, Jr.,
Abraham Tuttle,
Joshua Webb,
John White,
Nathan Wooley.

Roxbury.

Dr. David McClure,
Darius Spaulding,
Silas Spaulding.

Royalton.

David Ames,
Matthew Atherton,
Lyman Bache,
Stephen Backus,
John Billings,
Richard Bloss,
Lieut. Benj. Bosworth,
Samuel Cleveland,
Squier Cleveland,
Benjamin Cole,
Darius Dewey,
Ebenezer Dewey,
John Hutchinson,
Daniel Lovejoy,
Samuel Metcalf,
Benjamin Parkhurst,
Willard Pierce,
Isaac Pinney,
Daniel Rix,
Jeremiah Rust,
Isaac Skinner,
Elias Stevens,
Samuel Stewart,
Daniel Sumner,
Zachariah Waldrow,
Abraham Waterman,
Sergt. Wm. Waterman,
Silas Williams.

Rupert.

John Blanchard,
Isaac Clapp,
Levi Doane,
Enoch Eastman,
Israel Hayes,
John Parker,
Moses Sheldon,
Enoch Sherman,
Ashbel Sykes,
Harry Sykes,
Joel Taylor,
Daniel Warner.

Rutland.

Sgt. Tim'y Boardman,
Agel Cone,
Thaddeus Dunklee,
Moses Head,
John Johnson,
Nathan M.Loundsberry,
Nathan Osgood,
Sergt. Simeon Post,
Maj. Israel Smith,
Roswell Staples,
Artemas Taft,
Daniel Williams.

Ryegate.

Wells Goodwin,
Samuel Johnson,
Sylvanus Learned,
Allen Stewart.

Salisbury.

Stephen Rice.

Sandgate.

Abel Buck,
Asa Cogswell,
John Cogswell,
Adam Hurd,
John Wyman.

Shaftsbury.

Hezekiah Carey,
Aaron Denio,
Capt. Cyprian Downer,
John Fuller,
Giles Olin,
John Olin,
James Sweet,
Abiathar Waldo,
Prosper Wheeler.

Sharon.

Joel Barrett,
James Carpenter,
Ebenezer Currier,
Seth Hart,
Nathan Hitchcock,
Asahel Holt,
Benjamin Metcalf,
Oliver Sexton,
Reuben Spaulding,
Nicholas C. Wells.

Shelburne.

Phineas Hill,
Samuel Mills.

Sheldon.

Ebenezer Chamberlain,
Capt. Barth. Durkee,
Elim Gilbert,
Uriah Higgins,
Ruel Keith,
Joseph Lamb,
Josiah Peckham,
Ebenezer Stebbins.

Sherburne.

Joseph Adams,
Sergt. Amasa Fuller.

Shoreham.

Eliakim Culver,
Joel Doolittle,
Elisha Kellogg,
Stephen King,
Jonas Newton,
Lieut. John Smith,
Samuel Sunderland,
William Watson,
Jonathan Wilson.

Shrewsbury.

Jeffrey A. Barney,
Abram Eaton.

Somerset.

Elijah Morse.

South Hero.

Ephraim Holland.

Springfield.

Col. John Barrett,
Josiah Belknap,
Capt. Abner Bisbee,
John Bisbee,
William Bragg,
Elisha Brown,
Nathaniel Burgess,

Moses Chase,
Samuel Damon,
Stephen Dyer,
Samuel Dyke,
Joseph Ellis,
Oliver Fairbanks,
William Griffith,
Daniel Griswold,
John Griswold,
Levi Harlow,
Joseph Hulett,
Ephraim Lewis,
Jonathan Luke,
Lieut. Isaac Parker,
Silas Parker,
Jonas Pierce,
Sergt. Asahel Powers,
Jacob Sartwell,
Oliver Sartwell,
Samuel Shattuck,
Simeon Spencer,
Taylor Spencer,
Simon Stevens,
Moses Stickney,
David Stinson,
Isaac Tower,
Jed Ward,
Lemuel Whitney.

St. Albans.

Azariah Brooks,
Eleazer Brooks,
John Delaway,
Jehiel Holdridge,
John Mitchell,
David Powers,
Qm. Silas Robinson,
Jeremiah Virginia,
Solomon Walbridge.

Stamford.

Ira Hill,
Elisha Raymond.

Starksboro.

Abraham Hall,
Hebard Morrill,
Elisha Norton,
Ezekiel Pease.

St. George.

Joseph Doane.

St. Johnsbury.

Samuel Clark,
Jedediah Coe,
Comfort Healey,
Oliver Phelps,
Reuben Spaulding,
Isaac Stowell.

Stockbridge.

Stukely Angell,
John Durkee,
Sergt. Elias Keyes,
Jonathan Norris,
Walter Pollard,
Daniel Ranney.

Stowe.

Adam Alden,
Joseph Bennett,
Joseph Churchill,
Aaron Clough,
Nehemiah Doane,
Daniel Fuller,
Asa Kimball,
Abraham Moses,
William Pettengill,
Lieut. Martin Pitkin,
Asa Poland,
Noah Robinson,
Paul Sanborn,
Lieut. David Thomas,
Moses Thompson,
Elisha Town,
James Town.

Strafford.

Jethro Batchelder,
Nathan Cobb,
Edward Filch,
Nathaniel Morrill,
Aaron Pennock,
Benjamin Preston,
John Reynolds.

Stratton.

Jonathan M. Bissell,
Amos Parsons.

Sudbury.

Jesse Tenney.

Sunderland.

Capt. Lemuel Bradley,
John Rowen.

Swanton.

Peter Barsha,
John Pratt.

Thetford.

Bethuel Bryant,
Asa Corser,
Reuben Dickinson,
Jeremiah Dodge,
Azriah Faxon,
James Lock,
Beriah Loomis,
Bethuel Newcomb,
Leonard Robinson.

Tinmouth.

Isaac Libby,
Edmund Luens,
Col. Isaac Putnam,
Thomas Rogers,
David Spafford,
Orange Train.

Townshend.

George Austin,
Eleazer Cobleigh,
Bagalee Frost,
Sergt. Amos Gray,
Capt. John Livingston,
Thomas Lowe,
Jonathan Shattuck.

Troy.

Cyrus Allen.

Tunbridge.

Benjamin Adams,
William Ballou,
Jonathan Foster,

13

Daniel Hackett,
Enoch Hoyt,
Joseph Hoyt,
Ichabod King,
Nathan Noyes,
John Selly,
William White,
William Wright.

Underhill.

Samuel Calhoun,
Asa Rider,
Josiah Sheldon.

Vergennes.

Noah James,
David Tyler.

Vernon.

Jabez Clark,
Benjamin Lee,
Jesse Lee,
Elijah Stebbins.

Vershire.

Moses Bartholomew,
Samuel Comstock,
Enos Flanders,
Lemuel Southwick.

Waitsfield.

Samuel Barnard,
Abijah Brown,
Moses Chase,
Caleb Colton,
Thomas Green,
Joseph Hamilton,
Ezekiel Hawley,
Lieut. John Heaton,
Jesse Mix,
William Newcomb,
Joseph Osgood,
Jonathan Palmer,
Bissell Phelps,
Samuel Pike,
Lemuel Richardson,
Phineas Rider,
Salma Rider,

Amasa Skinner,
Jared Skinner,
Salah Smith,
Daniel Taylor,
Elias Taylor,
Ezra Wait,
Jeduthun Wait,
William Wait.

Walden.

Nathan Barker,
Elisha Cate,
Benjamin Dow,
Nathaniel Dow,
Nathaniel Perkins,
Timothy Shurtleff.

Wallingford.

Asa Anderson,
Philbrook Barrows,
Eli Calkin,
Sgt. Nathan Dennison,
Cyrenius Dewey,
Jerathunel Doty,
Andrew Hewitt,
Nathaniel Keyes,
Philip White.

Waltham.

John Preston.

Wardsboro.

Elisha Allen,
Pearley Fairbanks,
Sergt. Silas Gates,
Daniel Harris,
Sergt. Rufus Harvey,
Abner Lewis,
Ebenezer Pierce,
Aaron Rawson,
Thomas Simpson,

Warren.

William Chase.

Waterford.

John Chaplin,
Samuel Hill,
Moses Huntley,

John Melendy,
Thaddeus Potter.

Waterville.

Daniel Morse.

Weathersfield.

Jewett Boynton,
Col. John Boynton,
Isaac Brown,
Oliver Chamberlin,
John Chase,
Asa Grout,
John Haskill,
Samuel Holmes,
Abner Jackman,
Caleb Litchfield,
John Mallord,
William Nichols,
Moses Peabody,
Thomas Prentiss,
Stephen Reed,
Col. Elijah Robinson,
Clark Toles,
Benjamin Worcester.

Wells.

Ebenezer Butts,
Andrew Clerk,
Roswell Clark,
Stephen Clark,
John Davis,
Jonathan Francis,
Nathan Francis,
Rufus Glass,
Daniel Goodsell,
Samuel Goss,
Joshua Howe,
Samuel S. Merriam,
Hallowell Merrills,
James Paul,
Gould Stiles,
Jason Tyler.

West Fairlee.

Cephas Child,
Samuel Morison,
William Morris,
Maj. John Simpson.

Westfield.

Medad Hitchcock,
Benjamin Stebbins,
Bethuel Stebbins,

Westford.

Thomas Atwood,
Sylvester Crandal,
Isaac Gale,
Jesse Ide,
David Sawyer.

West Haven.

Sergt. Isaac Cutler,
Augustus Pease.

Westminster.

Hezekiah Abby,
Samuel Adams,
Silas Burk,
Simeon Burk,
Barnabas Clark,
Scatto Clark,
Joshua Cone,
Samuel Cone,
Josiah Eaton,
Maverick Eaton,
Elisha Johnson,
Reuben Lippenwill,
Jabez Paine,
John Priest,
Elijah Ranney,
Thomas Ranney,
William Ranney,
Amaziah Richmond.

Weston.

Jeremiah Blanchard,
Henry Hall,
Nicholas Lawrence,
William Lee,
Gideon Pease,
Thomas Piper,
Samuel Proctor,
Ezra Ritter.

West Windsor.

Abel Adams,
Isaac Adams,
Lieut. Sam'l Myrick,

Jerome Sawin,
Joseph Wakefield,
Asa Worcester.

Weybridge.

Samuel Clark,
Thomas Dickinson,
Benjamin Hagar,
John Halsey,
Pliny Stannard.

Wheelock.

Abner Hoyt,
Edward Magoon,
Nehemiah Phillips.

Whiting.

Gershom Justin,

Whitingham.

Nathan Green,
David Jillson,
Samuel Parker,
Stephen Putnam.

Williamstown.

Samuel Adams,
Asa Hatch,
Elijah Whitney.

Williston.

Joseph Blish,
Ebenezer Bradley,
Martin Chittenden,
Zachariah Hart,
Lenard Hodges,
Daniel Isham,
Stephen Randall,
Parce Stearns.

Wilmington.

Calvin Bill,
Henry Chandler,
Barnabas Cushman,
Ezra Mudge,
Calvin P. Perry,
Daniel Rice,
Col. Wm. Williams.

Windham.

Edward Aiken,
Nathaniel Aiken,
Peter Aiken,
William Ellis,
John Gould,
David Howard,
Samuel Howard,
Neil Noyes,
Benjamin Pierce,
James Smith,
James White,
Abiel Whitman.

Windsor.

Israel Aiken,
John Blood,
Briant Brown,
Solomon Burk,
Nathaniel Cobb,
Nathan Coolidge,
Sergt. Thomas Cray,
Oliver Diggins,
Abel Fling,
William Gilkey,
Isaac Green,
Jonathan Hall,
——— Houghton,
William Hunter,
Stephen Jacob,
Reuben McAlister,
David Morison,
Oliver Osgood,
Simeon Pomeroy,
Rufus Root,
Andrew Spalding,
Alden Spooner,
Dr. Thomas Stearns,
Henry Stevens,
Samuel Stickney,
Nahum Trask,
Joseph Willis.

Winhall.

Daniel Benson.

Wolcott.

Jabez Newland.

Woodford.

Elkanah Danforth,
Ebenezer Temple.

Woodstock.

Jabez Bennett,
William Bennett,
Sergt. Jacob Bevins,
Moses Bradley,
Ephraim Brewster,
Lieut. Col. Ebenezer
  Bridge,
Joel Burbank,
John M. Call,
Barnabas Caswell,
Binney Cobb,
Sergt. William Cone,
Nathan Cook,
Timothy Cox,
Noah Crocker,
Standish Day,
Asahel Doubleday,
Josiah Dunham,
Simeon Dunham,
Samuel Dutton,
Sergt. Ephraim Eddy,
James Emerson,
Jonathan Farnsworth,
Arunah Fullerton,
Benjamin Green,
Zebedee Hackett,
Edmund Harvey,

James Howland,
Abraham Kendall,
Isaac Kendall,
Jacob Kendall,
Timothy Knox,
William Labaree,
George Lake,
Jonathan Lake,
Elisha Lord,
Frederick Mather,
William McCloy,
Joshua Nye,
Gershom Palmer,
Oliver Palmer,
Capt. Wm. Perkins,
William Perry,
Phineas Powers,
Stephen Powers,
William Powers,
John Ransom,
Lt. Richard Ransom,
William Raymond,
Jason Richardson,
Lysander Richardson,
Henry Roby,
Elijah Royce,
Joseph Safford,
Philemon Samson,
George Sampson,
Sylvanus Shaw,
Samuel Slayton,
Stephen Smith,
Abram Snow,
Gardner Spooner,
Andrew Thomas,
Seth Washman,
Benuel Williams,
Jesse Williams,
Phineas Williams,
Roger Williams,
Eleazer Wood,
Joseph Wood.

www.ingramcontent.com/pod-product-compliance
Lightning Source LLC
Chambersburg PA
CBHW070517090426
42735CB00012B/2825